W9-CHC-126

Theoretical Models and Personality Theory

THEORETICAL MODELS AND
PERSONALITY THEORY

EDITED BY

DAVID KRECH
University of California

GEORGE S. KLEIN
The Menninger Foundation

GREENWOOD PRESS, PUBLISHERS
NEW YORK   1968

Contents

THEORETICAL MODELS AND PERSONALITY THEORY

Preface

THE PRESENT symposium is developed around the central problem of "Theoretical Models and Personality Theory."

The rationale for the symposium is roughly this: Psychologists and others have always been looking for some way to avoid mere fact-gathering and have always tried to find a means of parsimoniously and fruitfully linking all sorts of data. This attempt to theorize and build models for the purpose of generating new questions about behavior and gaining new insights and understanding is not at all new, of course. But the issue of developing theories and models seems to be a particularly live one today since more and more interest areas which previously were regarded as disparate are overlapping one with another. Recent experimental studies as well as theoretical papers seem to indicate that psychiatrists, personologists, perceptionists, learning theoreticians, neurologists, and physiologists are using each other's techniques and reading each other's papers. We feel that this is a strategic moment, then, to take time out and discuss the rules of procedure and models which would make these contacts more economical and productive.

DAVID KRECH AND GEORGE S. KLEIN, *Editors*

The Problem of Personality and Its Theory*

GEORGE S. KLEIN   AND   DAVID KRECH
The Menninger Foundation   University of California

CONCERN with theory has probably never before so dominated the consciousness of contemporary psychologists as it seems to be doing today. The most cursory glance at current publication lists, symposia, and conferences in psychology suggests very strongly that now is the time for conceptual stock-taking, theory-weaving, and integration. Our intention here is to go back a bit over the ground along which personality theory has traveled, to examine certain portions of the array of concepts it has already accumulated, to distinguish essentials from possible clichés and to evaluate these concepts for their future usefulness. Finally, we will try to outline what is, in our opinion, a fruitful basis upon which to construct the requirements of a psychological theory that will encompass the intentions of personality theorists.

"PERSONALITY THEORY": A PROBLEM MISCONCEIVED

Perhaps the first and most fundamental cliché which is popular among personality theorists (and many other theorists) is the very term "personality theory," used to mean a body of theory which is somehow different from any other psychological theory. In allusions to "personality" there is still evident an implication that we are dealing with a distinct set of behaviors, a unique set of phenomena which have their own laws and their own specialists. Just as it is still popular to speak of the expert in "perception" or in "learning theory," so is it still popular to speak of the expert in "personality dynamics."

The separation of the field of personality from the rest of psychology probably derives from an early tendency in experimental psychology to parcel out its subject matter to different experi-

* This paper was written while the authors were visiting members of the Department of Social Relations, Harvard University, during the academic year 1950-51.

menters and even different laboratories. In time, since almost every experimenter was also something of a theorist, "small-package" theories were developed to deal with each group of data—perception, learning, motivation, etc. Each of these small-package theories conceived of the person as if he were constituted of various "subsystems," e.g. a subsystem of "thinking," of "perceiving," of "learning," and each of these subsystems was approached as if its activity followed laws peculiar to itself. This "functional atomism" was perpetuated by greater and greater refinement of generalization about these subsystems, and as more and more theorists and experimentalists acquired more and more vested interests in these miniature theories, encapsulation bred the belief that such systems were a "fact" of man's nature. If there was at any time the belief that "perception," "learning," "thinking" were useful merely as economies of classification with which to summarize the kinds of *problems* which a single organism commonly faced, this was quickly lost in the microscopic attention given to each realm. One couldn't see the person for the subsystems, and if the organism was considered at all, it was treated (implicitly) merely as a collection of subsystems or, even worse, of subapparatuses.[1]

Related to any one subsystem there were (and are) of course, differences in bias and theory. Each subsystem has its "S-R" theorists, its "Gestalt" theorists, its "Simple Association" theorists, and even its "Functionalists." However, all meet on the common ground of believing that they are all concerned with systems of response.[2]

In a sense the field of personality developed in protest against this atomism. But in its development it not only failed to challenge

[1] Within this conception, individual differences arising from variables of central controls which influence the functioning of subsystems could command only minor interest. To raise the question of whether individual differences pointed to laws of organization superior to those of the miniature "system" could only be meaningless within a conception that takes it as axiomatic that the organism is a congeries of autonomous subunits. It is not surprising therefore that the question of individual differences was rarely raised. In the refining of the parts the governing context of a larger system was by-passed.

[2] It may seem that the functionalist theories, since they deal with "purpose," would somehow be more concerned than the others with problems of the *unity* of functioning, the role of the particular subsystem in the total economy of the organism. This is, however, not true. Functionalists can be as separatist as any other theorists. Thus Ames (2), perhaps the most thoroughgoing contemporary functionalist, speaks of the "purpose of a percept" as if this were intrinsic in the perceptual process itself and were invariant from person to person.

the basic premise of separatism; as we shall soon see, it strength-
ened it. The "personologists" compounded the errors of the traditional "experimentalists." It was clear to some that the "laws" of
the classical subsystems did not encompass all that we need to
know about behaving man. People seemed to be different from one
another. People seemed to be self-consistent (and even incon-
sistency seemed to follow an individual pattern). People had individual *styles*. Concern with these matters, since it had no place in
traditional psychology, became a separate field of investigation—and
a separate subject matter. But the personologist was still a psychologist, and as a psychologist he accepted the misplaced concrete-
ness of current rubrics; he merely added still another subsystem
called "personality" with its special data: "traits." Here then is
paradox and irony: The personologist who was born under the
banner of the "Whole Man" lives out his theoretical life seeking
the laws of the *sub*system "Whole Man."

In short, then, the field of personality consisted of the residual
phenomena not encompassed by the small-package conceptions of
particular systems. Gathering momentum in "trait" conceptions
and borrowing concepts from literature, conversation, and typologies, personality theory veered even further away from the other
areas of psychology while accepting the notion that each psychologist could properly theorize about his own subject matter—auton-
omously and independently.

But though the above description may be valid as a historical
account, it does not apply to some of the more recent developments
in personality theory. The drive for systematization and unifica-
tion of concepts seems to be especially active in current personality
theorizing. The impetus behind this trend seems to come from
experimental psychologists, as well as from the personologists
themselves.

Within the field of personality there has been a gradual trend
toward more functional conceptions of traits. Disembodied traits
without relation to the major functions of man seem to have lost
their appeal. This is evident, for instance, in a recent trend toward
broadened conceptions of traits as "dispositional tendencies" which
determine and qualify the patterning of behavior (1). Descriptively this point of view is an advance over the older theories of

traits as "behavior bits." But all uniformly stop short of pinning down trait definitions to *specificities* of cognitive-motivational functioning. Because of this deficiency they cling to the descriptive lexicons of older conceptions which failed to make systematic contact with behavior *processes*—the only means by which any trait concept can create effective conceptual bridges across to the rest of psychology. As a result it is still too easy to think of traits, even in the broadened sense, as "different" kinds of behaviors. When, furthermore, the trait is used on occasion to "explain," as when the effect of a trait *upon* cognitive behavior is sought, the "explanation" spins into the circularity of accounting for behavior in terms of categories used to describe it.

Thus as a final development of this more recent trend, some personologists have come to realize that the problem of the "influence of personality traits" *upon* cognitive-motivational functions is essentially a pseudo-problem. Some personologists have seen that it is the organization expressed in responses to learning problems, perceptual problems, thinking problems, and feeling problems which in the last analysis is what we mean by personality. "Personality theory, far from being an independent island with its own isolated structure, is really deeply embedded in the data of all these fields" (11).

This change in orientation parallels what is happening within the field of experimental psychology itself. The boundaries between the various subsystems have become more permeable as theoretical developments within each of them required consideration of events in other subsystems. It is increasingly difficult to speak of "perception" without saying something about "motivation," or to speak of "learning" without adequate attention to "perception," and so on. Here too there are signs of dissatisfaction with the subsystem approach and signs of a groping toward some other, more unified, orientation.

All of these developments can be summarized by saying that it is more and more apparent that an adequate personality theory must be a thoroughgoing behavior theory and that all theories of behavior must be personality theories. No theory of perception which does not deal with the fundamental objectives of the personality theorists can add up to an adequate theory of perception, or behavior, or anything else. And these objectives are the discovery of *the most general regulatory principles which determine a person's responses and account for individual differences among people.* Personologists have always sought for the "laws" of the total functioning organism. Our criticism of personality theorists is not that they had the wrong objectives, but that they failed to seek answers to their questions in the data of psychology in general. Had they worked more with the same data which concern the experimental psychologists, we would have avoided much of the esoteric isolationism which has characterized personality theory and much of the lifelessness and artificiality which has characterized behavior theory. Seen as personality theory, the limitations of the Hullian system or the Gestalt system become more evident. To insist on a learning theory or a perceptual theory in its own right is to make a virtue of restriction. The search for organismic laws highlights the inevitable inadequacy of such small-package theories.

Dissatisfaction with the older separatism, then, seems to have become general. This dissatisfaction has taken several forms of expression all dominated by the insistent theme that the data of personality are somehow resident in the phenomena of all the previously segregated subsystems. Few of these recent attempts at reformulation, however, go beyond demonstrating the point. The construction of a unifying alternative framework which would sweep away the confusions engendered by the older rubrics is rarely a direct aim. Because of this deficiency some of the newer developments in personality research, in a curious way, proceed from the older divisions without negating them, and as is true of the patchwork nature of many compromises, they delay the concerted effort required for molding a genuinely unified theory. A brief discussion of three such approaches—highly interrelated—will make this point clearer.

SOME PITFALLS IN CURRENT THINKING ABOUT "PERSONALITY" AND BEHAVIOR

There is the *inductive-correlational* approach, which is characterized by correlating individual differences with "traits." Thus in Witkin's studies (18) the rationale seems to be that since individual differences occur even in such apparently simple behaviors as spatial orientation, there is the possibility that these individual differences are somehow generated by central traits. Similar variations should be observed in adaptive responses of the same organisms to other problem situations—visual perception, problem-solving, etc. There is merit in this approach. The attempt to view individual differences, even in so-called neutral perceptual situations, as genotypic instances of more general laws of personality meets head on the challenge of individual differences; it extends personality theory into new areas, and emphasizes the inadequacy of theories based solely upon "stimulus characteristics."

On reconsideration, however, this approach does not free itself from the older conception of personality as a set of events which correlates with other sets of events (9). Such correlations have, at the very most, the demonstrational value of pointing to consistencies within the person. They emphasize, in other words, the *need* for a unified theory, but they advance us very little toward such a theory. The hope in such an approach is that when the correlation returns are in, there will emerge the necessary concepts and theory which will make the correlations understandable. The inescapable difficulty is that this approach, in accepting the older concepts, obscures the facts, since the concepts will determine the form in which the data are cast. By failing to wipe the slate clean and starting from unitary constructs, such an approach perpetuates the use of poorly systematized clinical concepts as well as the cliché handed down to us by the older personologists that personality is a "determinant" which somehow "causes" and therefore is correlated with "other" events.

Another current approach has been labeled the *interactionist* approach. This approach takes the view that perception, learning, and feeling are separate systems but that they "interact." And here again we have a well-nigh useless cliché. Though it stresses the idea that there is an "intertwining" of functions, it offers no suggestion of what this interaction is, of how it comes about, and, even more basically, of who the partners in the interaction may be. "Personality factors" are said to "interact" with "perceptual factors." Another difficulty of this position is that the issue of individual differences is almost completely neglected. The search is for "laws of interaction among subsystems"; the people in whom these subsystems function are still on the periphery.

The third approach is one which seeks to unify "personality" and "other" determinants by suggesting that all behavior is determined by *autochthonous* and *behavioral* factors. In many ways this orientation is a protest against the Gestalt emphasis (and the S-R emphasis) upon the tyranny of the objective stimulus as the determinant of behavior. "Autochthonous" factors are roughly co-ordinated with the "objective stimulus"; the "behavioral" factors, with "personality." This approach has many of the merits and all the faults of the other two orientations, and in addition, it establishes a most confusing distinction. Since autochthonous factors—if they mean anything at all—must mean factors operating in the organizing process, there is almost no way in which an autochthonous factor can be differentiated from a behavioral factor, which also operates in the organizing process. This is the old attempt to differentiate between "outer" and "inner" stimuli while asserting all the while that no stimulus is a stimulus until it becomes part of the "inner stimulating condition"!

This distinction is essentially identical with the one fashionably drawn between "stimulus" and "organismic" determinants (6). This formulation conceives of a continuum of stimulus "constraints" upon response such that as these "constraints" are relaxed, "personality"—the organismic factors—comes in. This solution seems to be currently favored by some perception theorists forced to give ground to pressures to recognize that "motives influence perceptions." But it is also one too readily agreed to by personality investigators themselves. For them it seems a likely way to resolve the contradiction between seeming *universality* of response in some situations, and *variation* in others. Universality would, presumably, be a consequence of stimulus determinants; it thus becomes the concern of the "other" psychologies. But this division has encouraged personologists to fall into the error of developing generalizations about personality in stimulus terms. For instance, this point of view is reflected in the common reference to certain stimuli as "ambiguous," a designation which implies that ambiguity is a characteristic of a stimulus rather than of an *experience governed by regulative properties of the organism,* a point to which we will return later. It carries also the implication of a uniquely separate subsystem of response (organismic determinants) brought into play sometimes but not all the time.

It is possible to resolve the problem by a straightforward shift to the position that the organism is *always* "responsible" for its behavior. If we conceive of "requiredness" of response as a property not of stimulus constraint but of *the constraining condition of the responding system,* then both universality as well as variation in response can be provided for within a single scheme of organismic control. Univocality of and universality of experience are no less the outcomes of response properties of individual organisms than is ambiguity of experience. In fact, any explanation of univocality must necessarily answer the question of how the organism is set up to make this possible. By the same reasoning, "ambiguity" would be not a stimulus property but an experience engendered by what a regulatory system *does with* a stimulus. The focus of behavior laws would then shift from concern with stimuli to a frank regard for conditions of organismic control. This view allows for the possibility that a stimulus, depending on the conditions of the control system—how it "handles" a stimulus—may be at one time ambiguous or at another univocal in meaning.

This view, however, poses a difficulty. How can we define "stimulus"? From everything we have said it is clear that definition of stimulus in psychologically meaningful terms is impossible as long as we continue to regard a stimulus as something "outside" the responding organism. *The meaning of the stimulus is the response to the stimulus.* What can it possibly mean, therefore, to say that the response is "due to" or is a "reaction to" the stimulus as perceived or experienced by the subject? It seems to us that there is only one way to deal with the problem of stimulus definition: Restrict the word "stimulus" to its original meaning—an objective, physically defined affair. The data with which we must deal are (a) the physically defined stimuli and (b) all events in the organism. Nothing more. We must drop the illusory notion that we can define a stimulus psychologically, i.e., in terms of the meaning it has for the subject. Thus a stimulus cannot be a "sex-object" or a "threatening picture." That is what was meant when we said a moment ago that the focus of behavior laws must shift from a concern with stimuli to a concern with the conditions of organismic control. Lest the charge be made that this view offers no place for studies indicating how response is related to the stimulus, we must point out that, for evaluation of "reality testing," careful definition of the *physical* stimulus is still possible.

The confusion of distinguishing between "autochthonous" and "behavioral" factors is also very much akin to the "functional" and "organic" distinction encountered in older personality theorizing. Perhaps this latter confusion can best be shown by pointing to the absurdities to which it has led us so many times. Again and again personality theorists have argued the question of "organic" determinants of mental disease versus "functional" determinants, or in slightly more modern terms, of "somatic" versus "psychic" determinants. Just a moment's thought will indicate that this distinction asserts that the "functional" or the "psychic" refers to events which have no neurological or organic basis! Actually all of these old (and recent) arguments seem to boil down to this position: The healthy functioning of the healthy person is non-physiological; the unhealthy functioning of the sick person may or may not be physiological, for no one seems ever to have asked the question whether healthy functioning is "organic" or "functional."

All the approaches discussed above have this in common: Research instigated by them centers in the demonstration of inadequacies of previous theories and, more specifically, of inadequacies in the simon-pure separatist position. But all of those approaches are equally ill-equipped to deal with their unitary theory. Consequently, questions raised by them are often cast in antiquated forms and invoke nonessential issues. Their research results really demonstrate mostly the lack of a useful theory.

REQUIREMENTS FOR A THEORY OF BEHAVIOR

And what are some of the major requirements which a useful behavior theory must meet? It seems to us that any good behavior theory (or "personality theory") must meet two main criteria: it must be a unified theory of behavior and it must be, as is true of any good theory in science, an "explanatory" theory, one which goes beyond describing the phenotypically observable and is capable of generating new deductions.

A unified theory of behavior would, it seems to us, set its sights on the following aims which have crystallized from personality research.

1. *Adaptive responses: an axiomatic orientation.* The kind of theory of behavior we are advocating is one which views all behavior within the context of the total organism. This is another way of saying that all of the processes within the organism are "adaptive"; each function or behavior serves an *organismic purpose.*[3]

However, this is as dangerous a position to take as it is essential. Pratt (15) has stated that psychology asks about the "what" and "how," not the "why" of behavior. If by that statement he means that the purpose of behavior is not an explanation of it, we fully and enthusiastically agree. But we must not confuse the "why" question with the "purposive" answer. It is necessary to *ask* "What is the purpose?"; it is completely inadequate, however, to end our answer with a statement of the purpose. We raise the question "why" *only to discover "how" and "what" answers.*

Not only is the raising of "why" questions demanded by our theoretical orientation, it has also demonstrated its heuristic value. In biology, for instance, the discovery of internal secretions led to the positing of "functions" for the ductless glands. When this occurred, a new set of possibilities regarding the mediating mechanisms (the "how" and "what") of internal secretion was raised.

Some behavior theories have failed to ask the "why" question and thereby have lost the organism; some personality theories have failed to answer in terms of "how" and "what" and have thereby lost theory—explanatory theory. To take an instance of the latter type: The psychoanalytic concept of repression is a "purposive" *answer:* it is a statement of a certain intention which is evident in response—or lack of response. To account for a response in terms of repression is only to state the "function" of the response. *How* repression occurs—its mechanism—is the next and central question. If we use the concept of repression to raise questions of how the

[3] "At all events the most convinced representative of an ateleological point of view must admit that actually an enormous preponderance of vital processes and mechanisms have a whole-maintaining character; were this not so the organism could not exist at all. But if this is so, then the establishment of the significance of the processes for the life of the organism is a necessary branch of investigation" (3, p. 12).

organism is constructed to permit such an adaptive response, then we stand to gain much. To imply, as Else Frenkel-Brunswik (5) and others have, that we perceive in such-and-such a manner because it serves this or that defensive purpose amounts to at most the early stage of a theory; it raises questions which a fully adequate theory must eventually answer. In focusing upon "why" questions, nevertheless, such orientations as those of psychoanalysis and Tolman's purpose behaviorism have made their most important contributions toward the possibilities of a theory. This, then, is the first guiding proposition we would suggest for a useful behavior theory: *It must insistently view all the processes of the organism as adaptive and must just as insistently seek a basis for "how" and "what" explanations thereof.*

2. *Organismic principles of control as the focus of theory.* In speaking of organismic principals of control, we have in mind a conception of the organism as a regulatory system in the context of which the expression of function can be understood. A unified theory of behavior would specify the properties of this regulating system and its laws. We would need to assume also that such governing systems vary in their constants, an assumption necessitated by the frequent allusions in the literature to individual differences.

"Organismic controls" may be conceived of in various ways. Our thesis, which we shall attempt to support below, is that these organismic controls can be most adequately treated in terms of the physiological or neurological substrate of the person. One such organismic principle—cortical conductivity—has recently been proposed in an analysis of figural aftereffects observed in brain-injured by Klein and Krech (10).

If we continue to pursue systematically our search for properties of the regulatory system and its structures, the "organismic axiom" paid so much lip service by personologists through the years will become more than an article of faith and will provide the basis of a truly explanatory theory. It is in this sense too that we can give meaning to Stern's (17) belief that the person "as such" *can* determine and account for behavior without implications of a homunculus.

3. *The data of behavior theory must encompass "cognitive" and*

"motivational" determinants. We have said that a behavior theory should view all behavior within the context of the total organism, and that its laws should be organismic principles of control. These organizational constants, however, will appear through responses— through behaviors classically known as "perceptual" or "cognitive." But though a behavior theory must reckon with all forms of response, it need not do so under the older rubrics which come from a different conception of the problem of theory in psychology. Using the older terms to classify the purely "objective" situations confronting a person *may* have some value, but the emphasis must turn away from considering these as kinds of *behaviors* or kinds of responding *systems*. The very descriptive units which we use in dealing with our observable behavior must be derived from and oriented toward a unitary concept of behavior, and the explanatory principles must be *all-inclusive*.

It has been argued that this orientation is desirable, but impossible to achieve—at this stage of our science, anyway. It is difficult enough, the objection runs, to handle "perceptual" behavior alone; how can we possibly handle, simultaneously, all the other "behaviors"? This difficulty may be more apparent than real. How do we know that there are so many "behaviors" to juggle simultaneously in our organismic laws? Perhaps all we have done is to split man up into smithereens and then to raise the problem: How can we juggle these smithereens simultaneously? Perhaps all we need do from the outset is to refuse to split man up: The dictum "the whole is *simpler* than the sum of its parts" may be applicable here. An analogy may make this point a bit clearer. Klineberg (12) reports that the Eskimos have a large variety of words for our one word "snow," i.e., they distinguish between wet snow, dry snow, old snow, new snow, etc. Now suppose we were to ask an Eskimo scientist to give us a *unitary* theory of "snow." It is highly probable that our mythical Eskimo scientist would throw up his hands in despair. But such a problem would be relatively simple for our own scientists—a man who never did divide snow into an array of *genotypically* different substances. And so it is with behavior. It is quite possible that a new approach will show that we do not have a large variety of different kinds of behavior (perceptual, learning, conceptual, emotional, rational, etc.) but only five or three or two kinds of behavior.

The attempt to seek a unitary theory of behavior asserts, of course, that there is no unique set of personality data. From this assumption it follows that the exclusion of the data and experimentation of the classical or orthodox or experimental psychologist is not tenable. The nonsense syllable, the maze, the puzzle, the figure-ground drawing, the aesthesiometer are as valid devices for achieving information about personality constants as the TAT story or Rorschach card. It is the generalization about the organismic law that is the issue, and the efficiency with which we can achieve the generalization is the only criterion by which to judge the appropriateness of a method or a datum.

These, briefly, are the issues posed to behavior theory by the several currents of contemporary personality research.

THE REQUIREMENTS OF "UNDERSTANDING," "EXPLANATION," AND "SURPLUS VALUE"

And now we come to the second criterion we listed—a good behavior theory must have *explanatory* value. And here, of course, we enter the very dangerous area of the philosophy and logic of science and scientific method.

Philosophers, educators, and scientists have perhaps written more truth and nonsense about "The Scientific Method" than about any other single subject of common concern. We would suggest that there exists in this subject one simple rule by which the valuable can be distinguished from the useless. The rule is this: Any statement on scientific method which starts with "the scientist does . . ." is most probably true for most scientists at one time or another; any statement which starts with "the scientist never . . ." is most probably incorrect for most scientists at one time or another. The scientific method, in other words, is at some time or other all things to all scientists. There is no such thing as THE scientific method.

It is more accurate to speak of science as a kind of adaptive behavior resulting from the special assignment which a certain class of people set for themselves. The assignment for the scientist is to apply himself to a domain of events in order to achieve so much understanding of it that his control of it and the predictions he makes about it will occur with a minimum of surprise (i.e., "error"). Seeing the scientific effort as just another kind of adaptive response to a special problem, one easily sees that there can be no rules or presumptions that will be invariant from scientist to scientist; effective solution of this problem as of any other problem may be tried via manifold routes. In a sense the scientist sets his own rules, since he tends to follow the preferred course of adaptive response indicative of what we here call his "personality."

These remarks about the psychology of science are necessary preliminaries to our perspective of what "understanding" is in science. There are no fixed rules for guiding us to *how* to achieve effective understanding. It is possible to specify only what is meant by effective understanding. And of course it is helpful, necessary, and possible to understand the nature of "understanding"—to see clearly the properties of explanation so that our skills and dispositions as scientific personalities will not be spent on self-delusion.

It is fashionable to say that understanding consists of "description" and "explanation." But what is the problem of "understanding" in science? Our answer is that the problem of understanding arises always when a *correlation*—a regularity—is discovered. The observed correlation is definitely a contribution to understanding since it makes possible some degree of prediction and control. But, equally important, a correlation always poses new questions. This implies a fundamental point about relation of description and explanation which must be clearly understood. It is this: understanding occurs in the *form* of correlations of events, but because correlations *always* pose problems about links which are not themselves evident in the correlation at hand, the task of understanding is never exhausted. Since adequate description consists of observed correlations, and since understanding is an ever-expanding series of correlations, explanation must be merely description carried to yet another point in the chain of linked events—i.e., to as yet unobserved correlations. When the latter become susceptible of direct scrutiny, they are "described" and the problem of explanation is renewed. An adequate *theory* is one which encompasses all the known correlations within the most parsimonious scheme of constructs, and allows of new possibilities of correlations, i.e., it has *surplus value*.

To illustrate: Suppose I have discovered a high and reliable correlation between a set of observable events A and another set of observable events A'. Am I, as a scientist, satisfied with a statement of this correlation? No simple "Yes" or "No" answer can be given. Of course I am happy about such a discovery. But elated though I may be, and no matter how useful to science this correlation may prove to be, I will not be completely satisfied with the statement of the correlations if by "satisfied" is now meant that I will do no more work with A and A'. Or, to state the matter more conservatively, if I *am* satisfied, my fellow scientist will not be. Either he or I will say at some point: "This correlation is a valid *description* of the interrelationships between A and A'. But it does not tell us *why* A and A' vary concomitantly."

What then will make this discovery of mine something other than a description? What else must I do before I have a satisfying scientific explanation? Our answer, and we believe that the history of science will indicate that it has been the answer throughout that history, would be something like this: I will consent to call it quits only when I have added to the law (that observable event A varies in such-and-such a manner from observable event A') a statement about an event B where B has no apparent, no previously known, no necessarily "common-sense" relationship to events A and A'. If, for instance, you say that the longer a person remains in a dark room, the more acute does his brightness vision become, and that the acuity improvement is related to length of "dark adaptation" in such-and-such a manner, we shall consider this observation a scientific achievement, shall be elated with you by your discovery, but we shall immediately ask "Why?" If you now assert (with or without adequate data) that the longer a person remains in a dark room, the greater the rate of recovery of visual purple functioning in the retinal rods, and that the chemical reaction of bleached visual purple to darkness (as observed in a test tube) proceeds at the same rate as does the improvement of visual acuity of a dark-adapted subject, *then* we will call your statement a "scientific explanation." The reason we feel satisfied to call it an "explanation" is that we have linked our first observed correlation to another order of correlation. We have extended our "understanding" through yet another correlation. The explanatory process is of course not exhausted even at this point.

Soon after this "explanation"—the new correlation—is accepted or "demonstrated" as valid, almost the moment that happens, the scientist experiences a new unresolved tension, a new feeling of dissatisfaction with the state of his science, and applying the epithet "superficial description" to the *new* correlation goes off again on the search for a new variable, a new correlation which will lead him to "understand" why visual purple has given us just the correlation he has found. Today's basic explanation is the superficial description of tomorrow.

As the authors read the history of theories in science, this is the way many advances have occurred. Sometimes the words used are not "description" and "explanation." Sometimes the words used are "laws" and "theories," sometimes "effects" and "causes," sometimes even "superficial" and "intrinsic." But whatever the words, the sequence of events seems to have been about the same, in so far as *any* consistent pattern can be discovered in the history of science. Now, we are prepared to say that this sequential description is more than a story of how the scientist *has* operated. It is also a good way for the psychologist-scientist to operate. For if it is true that a legitimate working conception of "cause" is that it consists of links among events within the organism, then the ultimate objective of psychology is to know or to state the intimate web of all of these *interrelationships*. This means that every reliable correlation, every law, and every set of laws is an addition to science. But this also means that every correlation is inadequate and can be improved by complicating the correlational statements through the supposition of "new" correlations. The latter always add to the "reasonableness" of those already known.

We have given considerable attention to some of the critical features of "explanation" in order to divorce it from the usual harmful and misleading implications of "cause." The aim of explanation is to unfold patterns of regularity, which we conceive of as chains of event sequences continually in modification and interaction. Cause would be for us a hypothesis regarding such a chain of sequences and explanation merely adds to our picture of it as postulated through a theory. A correlation represents an "entrance" into this chain; it does not exhaust our picture of it, *and to go from correlation to correlation has no implication that we are going from one "level" of causes or "analysis" to another, or that we are approaching an "ultimate" determinant.*[4]

THE PROBLEM OF "UNITS OF ANALYSIS"

The clothing of correlations is always concepts—concepts which imply still further correlation. But which concepts? How shall we achieve *conceptual* order in describing organismic control principles —the chains of event sequences—and at the same time adhere to the requirements of explanation and surplus value?

There are really two problems for the theorist here: a general conception of what the functioning of the organism really comes to in its most general terms, and the choice of appropriate concepts to convey this generalized conception. Shall we fashion our model and our constructs somehow out of the stuff of phenomenology: "attention," "set," "feeling," etc.? Or shall we look to an electronic model—a mechanism which is presumed to embody the essence of organismic control—and use such constructs as "signal," "scanning," "noise," and "coding" in understanding human data? Or shall we restrict ourselves to a set of formal, mathematical statements of relationships among behaviors? These are only some of the proposals that have been made in psychology and that are now being exploited by both theorists and experimentalists.

As has already been indicated, we favor still another view, one which also has its proponents in current psychological thinking— the neural-physiological model. Hebb (**7, 8**) and Krech (**13, 14**) have recently discussed in detail the possible fruitfulness of such an approach for developing a comprehensive theory of behavior. It asserts, in brief, that physiological conceptions are the most congenial and direct units for describing the organism. Its argument goes: Psychological functions have no meaning apart from their

---

[4] What is the relation between this approach to explanation and the approach which phrases the problem in terms of "intervening variables" or "hypothetical constructs?" The latter formulation sees "hypothetical constructs" as processes which mediate *between* the stimulating conditions and the behavior. If we limit our definition of behavior to observable muscular behavior then there is no difference between our formulation of the "explanatory" problem and the "hypothetical construct" formulation; in both instances a chain of event sequence is involved and "hypothetical constructs" are seen as hypothesized additional sets of events in the looked-for pattern of regularity.

being events of the physiology of the organism. Psychological constructs are only *translations* of these. Since this is so, any purely psychological theory will require retranslation eventually for complete understanding to occur. This argument would hold for the mechanisms borrowed from electronics.

By using neurophysiological units as the language of description of these "intervening" events, we are merely recognizing that the *entire* behavior of the organism is to be seen as a series of physiological events some of which are neurological, some of which are muscular, some of which are glandular, etc. Here "neurological explanation" is nothing more than our recognition of a place in this event sequence at which we can most efficiently interfere for the purpose of encompassing eventually the entire sequence.

Now all proposed models recognize the need for reaching toward new and not obvious correlations. In this sense *any* additional intervening variable which is added to our formula represents a step ahead. But we must be careful here lest we fall prey to a not uncommon error in psychological theory. We must be certain that we have indeed added a "new" variable and widened our understanding of the chain of event sequences in accounting for a correlation—that we have not merely added "A" under a new name. For instance: Suppose we find that tachistoscopic recognition-time varies with the degree to which the stimulus evokes sexual connotations full of conflict. Suppose we now go one step further and "explain" that the recognition failure is the outcome of a process called "inhibition," or "repression," or "selective resonance." Suppose we even specify the properties of "inhibition." Now such specification will often include the statement that inhibition consists of recognition failure. Thus a property is defined in only slightly more general terms than the operation itself and we are lulled into believing that we have gone beyond it. Many so-called psychological intervening variables are of the same order, i.e., the "intervening variable" or the "explanatory variable" is nothing more than a *name* for the observed correlation or else is measured in terms of either the dependent or independent variable. Specification of "properties" in such views is on close inspection nothing more than specification of operations—a depressing circularity. The moral of this is simple. One should make certain that any "new" variable, and hence proposed correlation, is definable and measurable *independently* of the events observed in the original correlation. This suggests a good "rule of thumb": the further afield you go for your explanatory variables, the safer you are.

Now we suspect that no one will argue with our assertion that "purely neurophysiological" intervening variables are "new" variables, that they can be defined and measured independently of behavior or stimulus events, and that in so far as they can be demonstrated to "fit in" with any sequential correlational statement, their inclusion would mark a step forward in "explanation." At some time new "B" variables must be introduced in the chain of event sequences and among such "B" variables must be neurological events. But several objections may be raised to the attempt to do that now. Isn't it true, runs one argument, that we know so little about neurology and that we have so inadequate a description of behavior and stimulus-response correlations that we can eschew "explanation" and stick to "description" for a while yet—a long while? This seems to be the position held by Rapaport (18) and others. We must confess that this is a difficult question to answer, and essentially it is a matter of judgment as to scientific tactics. Our judgment is obvious: we feel that it is never too early for speculation and theory in science. We don't believe, of course, that everyone should immediately become a neurologizing psychologist, but "now" is always the time for *some* of us *some* of the time to do so.

We also feel that neurology has much to gain from neurologizing psychologists, that the inadequacy of neurology will be remedied in part by the attention the neurologist pays to psychological data and theory, and if he is slow to attend, then we psychologists must. Finally, we feel that the game of neurologizing has already paid off. Here we would point to the theories of Koehler, Lashley, Hebb and Goldstein.

It is sometimes heard that purely psychological constructs commit us to less, are less speculative, more faithful to phenomenology, and because of this, are less restrictive and violate experience less; whereas neurological constructs are more speculative and dull our psychological sensitivity. To this objection we answer: theories are always speculative; a judgment of "more" or "less" speculation is not the yardstick for distinguishing them. More important, the requirement that theory should "stay close to experience" means only that it should encompass what is reported by descriptions of behavior. A good neurological theory must take that fidelity as its first responsibility and should *deepen* rather than constrict our understanding of experience and behavior. It should give us a more effective means of encompassing more and more aspects of the "phenomenological field." The failure of past and of most present neurological theories to do this is not a failure only of them but of "psychological" ones too. Inadequate theories, of whatever ilk, are inadequate.

There *is* a difficulty in applying neurological constructs. This is the problem of generating deductions about *observed* behavior —the problem of "transform operations." In recognizing this to be a problem for a neurological model, again we must point out that the problem is not unique to it: such "psychological" constructs as "anticipation" or "hypothesis" have similar troubles. One way out for neurological models is to postulate an *identity* between details of physiological process and observed behavior. For instance, it can *postulate* that certain forms of experienced "memory" phenomena consist of a process of communication between cortical loci (with the properties of communication and loci spelled out). The setting up of "memory" experiments will be guided by this assumption.

There is another kind of objection raised to neurological models. This is the position stated so clearly by von Bertalanffy (4) when he points out: "We can either build hypothetical constructs in the form of assumed entities; or we can try models that are noncommittal with respect to the entities concerned, and only give a formalization of the laws of the phenomena under consideration." And he would assign neurological constructs, of course, to the first type. That the second type is useful and fruitful he demonstrates by pointing out that "Mendel's original system was a 'formal' theory. It gives the laws of distribution of hereditary characters in successive generations of hybrids, but Mendel knew nothing about chromosomes, meiosis, haploid and diploid cells and so forth. . . ." There are two answers to this. In the first place, as von Bertalanffy himself points out, Mendel knew nothing about the material basis of heredity. But we *do* know something about the "material" basis of behavior. We do know, or think we know, that behavior is very intimately dependent upon the functioning of the nervous system. There is no need for us to pretend ignorance and to insist on building our model with a maximum degree of freedom. We cannot avoid the responsibility which Mendel was forced to avoid. In the second place, we would repeat Hebb's (8) observation: To pretend that in our "formal" model we were not referring to neural events might prove very dangerous. Consciously or unconsciously even our most formal models would reflect our notions about neurology, and because these notions would be "unconscious" or "concealed," they might very well be the "wrong," the least useful notions.

FINAL PERSPECTIVE

In the present paper we have retraveled a winding road of theoretical aspiration which reaches toward a conception of organismic control. Our purpose was to see where new extensions might be pushed most profitably and to point out needless and uneconomical detours it has previously taken. We have tried to formulate a number of guide-signs designed to assess any theory of behavior and to keep us clearly focused upon our aim, direction signs which may insure that a theoretical product will answer to the aspirations of personologist and behavior theorist. We ask about each: How does it confront the problem of explanation and with what units of analysis? Does it have surplus value in the sense of truly pointing to *new* sets of regularities rather than merely restating and renaming the known? Are organismic principles of control the focus of inquiry? Does it center on clarification and explanation of *adaptive* responses, and the variations occurring in them? Is it a unitary theory in that it encompasses all behavior data—the so-called cognitive and motivational?

REFERENCES

1. ALLPORT, G. W. *Personality: a psychological interpretation.* New York: Henry Holt, 1937.
2. AMES, A., JR. *Nature and origin of perceptions.* Preliminary laboratory manual for use with demonstrations disclosing phenomena which increase our understanding of the nature of perception. Hanover, N. H.: The Hanover Institute (unpublished).
3. BERTALANFFY, L. VON. *Modern theories of development.* Trans. by J. H. Woodger. London: Oxford Univ. Press, 1933.

4. BERTALANᶠFY, L. VON. Theoretical models in biology and psychology. *J. Personal.*, 1951, **20**, 24-38.

5. FRENKEL-BRUNSWIK, ELSE. Personality theory and perception. In R. R. Blake and G. V. Ramsey (eds.), *Perception: an approach to personality*. New York: Ronald, 1951.

6. GRAHAM, C. H. Visual perception. In S. S. Stevens (ed.), *Handbook of experimental psychology*. New York: John Wiley & Sons, 1951.

7. HEBB, DONALD O. *The organization of behavior*. New York: John Wiley & Sons, 1949.

8. HEBB, DONALD O. The role of neurological ideas in psychology. *J. Personal.*, 1951, **20**, 39-55.

9. KLEIN, G. S. The personal world through perception. In R. R. Blake and G. V. Ramsey (eds.), *Perception: an approach to personality*. New York: Ronald, 1951.

10. KLEIN, G. S., AND KRECH, D. Cortical conductivity in the brain-injured. To be published.

11. KLEIN, G. S., AND SCHLESINGER, H. J. Where is the perceiver in perceptual theory? *J. Personal.*, 1949, **18**, 32-47.

12. KLINEBERG, OTTO. *Social psychology*. New York: Henry Holt, 1940.

13. KRECH, D. Dynamic systems, psychological fields, and hypothetical constructs. *Psychol. Rev.*, 1950, **57**, 283-90.

14. KRECH, D. Dynamic systems as open neurological systems. *Psychol. Rev.*, 1950, **57**, 345-61.

15. PRATT, C. C. *The logic of modern psychology*. New York: Macmillan, 1939.

16. RAPAPORT, D. The conceptual model of psychoanalysis. *J. Personal.*, 1951, **20**, 56-81.

17. STERN, W. *General psychology from the personalistic standpoint*. New York: Macmillan, 1938.

18. WITKIN, H. A. The nature and importance of individual differences in perception. *J. Personal.*, 1949, **18**, 145-70.

Theoretical Models in Biology and Psychology

LUDWIG von BERTALANFFY

Department of Biology, Faculty of Medicine, University of Ottawa

---

Necessity and Limitations of Model Conceptions

In a consideration of theoretical models the first question is whether such models are necessary and desirable at all. Empiristic movements have often answered in the negative. History of science shows, however, that progress does not consist in a mere gathering of facts, but largely depends on the establishment of theoretical constructs. Idealizations never completely realized in nature, such as the conceptions of an ideal gas or an absolutely rigid body, and constructs such as the structural formulae in chemistry or the planetary model of the atom, form the basis of physical theory. On the other hand, the fact that adequate model conceptions have not yet been found is the reason that many fields within the biological sciences are a mere collection of an ever increasing amount of data, lacking exact laws and not permitting control of the phenomena in thought and in practice.

Though the necessity of theoretical models may be granted, we must be aware of their limitations also, especially as far as psychology is concerned.

Theoretical constructs are essentially a means of establishing "laws of nature." A first limitation can be expressed by the dictum of the scholastics: *individuum est ineffabile*. All laws of nature are essentially of a statistical character; that is, they are statements about the average of a great number of events. This fact is understood in physics, where micro-events at the level of the elementary units are unpredictable in principle, whereas the seemingly deterministic laws of macrophysics result from the average behavior of a practically infinite number of elementary units. The same dictum holds true, a fortiori, for the higher levels of reality. We are able to state laws in the fields of biology, behavior, and sociology which are essentially laws of the average behavior of biological units on the cellular, organismic, and superorganismic levels. Here, however, a peculiar situation arises. Our interest in the individual is at a minimum with physical entities, and so the statistical law gives us all the information we want. Amoebas, earthworms, and even dogs as far as they are objects of the physiologist's research, are almost physical objects. *My* dog, however, and even the planaria which became familiar to me during some time of observation, are individuals. With human beings, our interest in the individual is at the maximum. It is true that we are able to establish exact laws even here for average behavior. For example, it is an empirical law that so many persons are killed per year in car accidents or are murdered, and demography, insurance statistics, national economy, etc. present highly elaborated systems of laws, based upon suitable model conceptions. However, our interest in human beings is not satisfied by knowing these statistical laws; we feel that another type of insight is necessary, namely, to understand the individual, as it is expressed, in the highest form, in the work of the great artist and poet. This is the antithesis between "nomothetic" and "idiographic" attitudes, between "scientific" and "understanding" psychology *(verstehende Psychologie)*, which may be indicated by a diagram:

IDIOGRAPHIC ATTITUDE

PHYSICAL OBJECTS 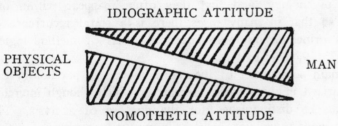 MAN

NOMOTHETIC ATTITUDE

FIG. 1: Diagrammatic representation of nomothetic and idiographic attitudes.

Scientific psychology is concerned with the first attitude, and it is to it that model conceptions belong.

The second limitation of model conceptions in psychology is a consequence of the fact that "inner" or "mental" experience constitutes a level of reality different from that of "outer" or "physical" experience. Our inner experience, perceptions, emotions, decisions of will cannot be reduced to action currents, hormones circulating in the blood, switching of excitations over certain synapses, and the like. The best we can hope for is to find, as far as certain aspects are concerned, a formal correspondence or isomorphy between the laws characterizing the processes in the nervous system and those found in mental phenomena. "The unity of science will not be achieved by *reducing* psychological principles to neurological ones, and neurological ones to physical ones. What we must seek is to make physical principles *congruent* with neurological ones, neurological ones with psychological ones" (14, p. 246).

As one bears in mind these limitations, the next step is to decide in what direction theoretical models in psychology should be sought. The situation is similar to that existing when, twenty-five years ago, an effort was made to determine, by examination of the fundamental explanatory schemes in morphogenesis, the necessary orientation in biology (2). Since the present author is a biologist, it appears that a demonstration of the parallelism in the modern trends of psychology and biology should be the main task of his contribution. More detailed discussions have been given elsewhere (4, 5).

Actually, the number of conceptual schemes available for the interpretation of reality is rather restricted. So it is no wonder that corresponding schemes appear in different fields, such as biology and psychology, and that they often reappear within one science, "so that in many cases there is a spiral recurrence of analogous principles on more advanced levels of methodological perfection" (10, p. 75).

The main possibilities of theoretical models in psychology can be summarized in three basic alternatives which, though interconnected, can be distinguished for the purpose of analysis. The antithetic models are not necessarily mutually exclusive; rather they represent complementary and different, but equally necessary approaches.

FIRST ALTERNATIVE: STATIC AND DYNAMIC MODELS

The basic characteristic encountered in biological as well as in psychological phenomena, considered from both the behavioristic and introspective standpoints, is the order and pattern of events. To explain order, there are two fundamental possibilities. The first is explanation in terms of *structural arrangements;* the second is explanation in terms of *dynamic interaction of processes.*

The first alternative is, of course, represented by the classical neuron, center, localization, and association theory. The pattern of the neural, and corresponding mental, processes is granted by the architecture of the nervous system. The centers represent relays or switchboards connecting incoming stimuli and excitations going out to the effectors; they are, therefore, fixed "machines" for definite functions. There is a point-to-point correspondence between, say, the excitation of elements of the retina, of the corresponding nerve cells in the visual cortex, and of elementary sensations the sum of which represents perception. Memory, association, the establishment of conditioned reflexes, etc., are based upon the building-up of nerve-paths between neurons and centers.

The criticism of classical theory as given by Gestalt theory need not be repeated here. It should be mentioned, however, that some important aspects of Gestalt phenomena can well be accounted for in more refined structural theories. Rashevsky indicated in 1931 (**19, 20**), a model of a thinking machine capable of gestalt discrimination, and, more recently, Cybernetics has offered a new theory of neural mechanisms in general and gestalt discrimination in particular. According to Wiener (**23**), *Gestalten,* e.g. different perspective views of a figure recognized as the same, form a transformation group in the sense of group theory. As in ordinary television a two-dimensional plane is covered by the process of scanning, so every region in a group-space of any number of dimensions can be represented by a process of group-scanning whereby all positions in this space are traversed in a one-dimensional sequence. Such a process can serve as a method of identifying the shape of a figure independently of its size, its orientation, or other transformations, and is well adapted to mechanization. A device for group-scanning, planned as a prosthesis for the blind and registering the *Gestalten* of printed letters by means of photoelectric cells and an arrangement of tones of different pitch, was developed by McCulloch. The scheme of this arrangement resembles the arrangement of neurons and nerve connections in the fourth layer of the visual cortex.

But there are other facts that can hardly be reconciled even with a refined machine model and that are indicative of a genuinely dynamic order.

The first is the *principle of closure*. If incomplete figures, as, for example, a circle with a little gap, are presented in the tachistoscopic experiment, movements of closure are seen; the free ends of the figure seem to flash together. Or if a number of points in circular arrangement are presented with one point somewhat outside the circle, this point appears to move into the periphery in order to complete the circle according to the "law of pregnance." Phenomena of this kind, many well-known examples of which are offered in Gestalt theory, unmistakably show a dynamic order.

Secondly, there is a principle which is very characteristic of biological and psychological phenomena and which may be called the *principle of progressive segregation* (**5, 7**).

Hierarchical order in physical systems, as, for instance, the space-lattice of a crystal, results from the union of originally separate systems of lower order, atoms in this case. In contrast, in the biological realm primary wholes segregate into sub-systems. . . . Classical association psychology assumes that individual sensations, corresponding to the excitation of individual receptor elements, for example of the retina, are the primary elements, and that they are integrated into perceived shapes. However, modern research makes it probable that at first there are yet unorganized and amorphous wholes which progressively differentiate. This is shown in pathological cases. With patients recovering after cerebral injuries, it is not punctual sensations that reappear first. A point-light causes, at first, not the sensation of a luminous point, but of a vaguely circumscribed brightness; only later on, perception of shapes and finally of points is restored. Similar to embryonic development, the restoration of vision progresses from an undifferentiated to a differentiated state, and the same probably holds true for the phylogenetic evolution of perception. (**5**, p. 52)

Thirdly, there is the body of *neurological experience* which presents two antithetic aspects. On the one hand, there is the vast amount of evidence upon which center and localization theory is based. The study of the responses and activities of isolated parts of the central nervous system, of the loss of functions after pathological or experimental injuries, and of localized stimulations leads to the classical picture of segmentally arranged reflex centers in the spinal cord, of reflex and automatic centers in the medulla oblongata, and of sensory, motor, and association fields in the brain. On the other hand, there is the clinical and experimental evidence for regulation, indicating the equipotentiality and functioning as a whole of the nervous system. Bethe's experiments (**8, 9**), for example, have shown that motoric co-ordination is re-established after amputations and thus is controlled not by pre-established central mechanisms, but rather by the entire complex of conditions present at the periphery and in the C.N.S. according to dynamic laws which have been elucidated, especially in the more recent work of von Holst (13). Lashley's (17) and Krech's (15) experiments on rats as well as Goldstein's (12) clinical observations show that localized brain injuries lead to a general deterioration of behavior and mental abilities rather than to the loss of individual functions.

Possibly the most obvious demonstration that the brain functions as a whole is "narrowness of consciousness." The fact that only one experience is in the focus of consciousness at a time seems to indicate that its physiological correlate extends over the whole "brain field." If the mosaic theory were correct, obviously any number of excitations and corresponding experiences could be co-existent.

The theory of memory probably also must be reshaped in a similar way. Here too, the classical conception was summative and mechanistic, assuming that traits or engrams of former excitations are deposited in small groups of ganglion cells, connected by myriads of nerve connections. If, however, form perception is a system process, dynamically ordered and extended over larger brain areas, the after-effect of excitation will consist not in leaving traits in individual cells, but in an alteration of the brain-field as a whole. Experimental and clinical facts indicate that the brain does not work as a sum of cells or sharply circumscribed centers; after brain lesions, never a single function is lost, but always others are impaired, the more the higher their demands on brain function. Thus another explanation presents itself as opposed to path theory: The process in the brain during the period of learning, when two stimuli were co-existent, represents a unitary whole; after fixation, a partial stimulus will lead to the revival of the trait as a whole, and thus to association, recognition, and conditioned reflex. (5, pp. 178-179, cf. also 21)

Thus, it is necessary to see whether it is possible to find a common denominator for the two contradicting lines of evidence and the antithetic model conceptions derived therefrom.

Progressive Mechanization

Such solution seems to be possible. Progressive segregation means, at the same time, progressive mechanization, a principle encountered in many biological phenomena.

Primarily, organic processes are governed by the interplay within the entire system, by a dynamic order, and this is at the basis of regulability. Secondarily, progressive mechanization takes place, that is, the splitting of the originally unitary action into individual actions occurring in fixed structures. . . . The C.N.S. progresses from a less mechanized to an increasingly more mechanized state though this mechanization is never complete as shown by regulation. Phylogenetically, a progressive fixation of centers can be found in the series of vertebrates. . . . Similarly, ontogenetic investigation shows that not local reflexes are the primary element of behavior, as upheld by classical theory, but that they rather differentiate from primitive actions of the body as a whole or of larger body regions. (5, pp. 29, 113)

This conception accounts for what is called by Krech (14) the different degrees of "rigidity" of the dynamic systems of the brain. On the other hand, Krech's finding that the behavior of rats with brain lesions is more stereotyped than that of normal rats and that they show less initiative than do normal rats (15) seems to be a consequence of the fact that it is particularly the higher functions which demand intactness of the brain.

Mechanization is, of course, even more familiar in the behavioral and mental realms when activities that are plastic and under conscious control at first become fixed and unconscious, as is the case in every process of learning, from the development of the child's motoric reactions to car-driving, playing the piano, and learning differential calculus. Actually, the classical explanation of learning by way of the establishment of nerve connections implies that there is at first a yet undifferentiated system where such connections can be established. Progress is possible only by mechanization; it can be achieved only by differentiation, specialization, and establishment of mechanisms that carry through the function in a fixed way and thus with minimum expense. On the other hand, this implies the fatal character of every evolution: for mechanization must be paid for by loss of versatility, and it nips other possibilities.

It is a consequence of progressive mechanization that the machine model is especially fit for the explanation of rational thinking. Reasoning according to the laws of logic and the conceptual system of mathematics is actually something like a thinking machine. We put in certain premises, the machine runs according to fixed rules, and the result drops out. Discursive thinking proceeds along a fixed path of decisions between alternatives, after the fashion of two-valued logic and the binary system applied in modern calculating machines. This conception is much less appropriate, on the one hand, for everyday experience and behavior, which depends on the status of the psychophysical system as a whole, and in which cognition is interwoven with all sorts of co-existing perceptions and emotional and affective factors, and on the other, for creative thought. The dependence of perception on the context of experience has been most impressively shown in the work of Ames, Cantril, and their group, and so it is no wonder that they come to "transactional" conceptions and, in their general outlook (11), to a standpoint closely related to organismic biology. The electronic brain and the brain as a calculating machine will be able to solve problems to which the machinery was set; it will not be capable of autonomous re-setting, of breaking the old rules and making new ones, of inventiveness and creativeness (cf. 10, pp. 134-135).

It is perhaps the profoundest objection against Cybernetics—as it is, at another level, against Descartes—that "thinking" proper, and the corresponding neural mechanism, is not a primeval function, but rather a late product of evolution.

CLOSED AND OPEN SYSTEMS

It appears, therefore, that the primary principle of neural order is to be sought in dynamics. Fixed centers, paths, and localizations are established in progressive mechanization, structural order thus gaining an ever higher significance and allowing for interpretation in terms of machine models. This is, of course, substantially the platform defended by Gestalt theory. However, certain qualifications have to be made.

Koehler tries to explain organic regulations by the attainment of states of equilibrium resulting from the Second Law of thermodynamics. But this conception is inapplicable, in principle, to the living organism, because it is not a system in thermodynamic equilibrium, but an open system kept at distance from equilibrium. Therefore, the development of a theory of organic order and regulation asks for new principles to be given by the theory of open systems. (5, p. 181)

Thus it appears that neurophysiological *Gestalten* are to be considered as "open" rather than as "closed" systems. The physico-chemical and biological theory of open systems has been outlined elsewhere by the present author (6) and its bearing for psychology was discussed by Krech (14). Here only a few consequences will be indicated.

One of the basic principles of Gestalt theory is the *law of pregnance*, stating that perceived *gestalten* tend towards the maximum regularity, symmetry, and simplicity possible under the circumstances and considered to be a consequence of the attainment of states of equilibrium in the corresponding neurophysiological *Gestalten*. As Krech emphasizes, an open-system model in neurophysiology "suggests that some experienced forms, under some circumstances, may tend toward *increased* heterogeneity and *increased* complexity" (14, p. 353). Possibly the open-system character is responsible for an essential feature of biological and psychological systems, namely, that their organization is established by way of segregation and differentiation of originally homogeneous wholes (cf. also 16). This statement is certainly true of biological phenomena as, for instance, ontogenesis, where increasing organization is possible only through expense of energy, and thus in open systems. It may be that the same point of view should be applied to neurological theory.

Another important consequence of the theory of open systems is *equifinality*. Whereas in the familiar closed systems of physics the final state is determined by the initial conditions, in open systems, as far as they attain a steady state, this state can be reached from different initial conditions and in different ways; it is thus equifinal (6). This definition corresponds to that of "vicarious functioning" in behaviorism (Hunter, Boring, Brunswik, and others), that is, the reaching of the same goal by different means, which is considered to be a major characteristic of behavior and mental activities and a main objection against mechanistic models. Probably "vicarious functioning" is a collective term, including phenomena of different kinds. One possibility is based upon progressive segregation (see above). It appears that centers are not machineries fixed from the beginning, but that they differentiate in a process of progressive mechanization. Thus a center is not a sharply circumscribed region; its functional potencies usually extend over larger parts of the C.N.S. In the normal course of events that region which can do it best governs the function; it is the leading part. If this region is injured, other parts which have the same potency, though to a lesser extent, may do the job and thus give rise to vicarious functioning. Another part of vicarious functioning may be taken care of by feedback mechanisms. If, for example, the same goal can be reached by different ways of locomotion such as running, flying, swimming, etc., then, as in a guided missile possessing different kinds of locomotor apparatus, the effect may be due to a switching-over from one type of locomotion to another, each feedback-controlled, and thus lead to the effect mentioned. Finally, there may be phenomena of vicarious functioning which are due to true equifinality, that is, attainment of the same steady state from different initial conditions.

Another main objection against the classical stimulus-response scheme is that it considers the organism as a reactive system, comparable to a penny-in-the-slot machine which is put into action only by external influences. In contrast, modern research leads to consideration of the organism as an essentially *active system*. It appears that autonomous function, as exemplified by the activity of rhythmic-automatic centers, is to be considered as primary, and upon it the reactive mechanism of the reflexes is superimposed as a secondary regulating device (3, 5, 13). Similarly, automatic sequences of impulses, the so-called hereditary co-ordinations which are often discharged without even external stimuli, play a predominant role in instinctive behavior (18). In contrast to machine theory, this primary activity is one of the essentials of organismic biology in general, and of the theory of the organism as an open system in particular. The organism appears as a flow of processes which can be considered, for certain purposes and in a first approximation, to be in a steady state. Superimposed on the steady state are smaller process waves, a rhythmical storing and discharge of impulses after the type of relaxation oscillations which give rise to autonomous activities and to rhythmic-automatic functions in particular.

The consideration of the organism as an open system has important consequences in physics and biology. It is to be noticed that virtually all leading schools of behaviorism and psychology are based upon theories of the closed-system type. This fact has been well expressed by Brunswik:

Re gestalt theory: The frame of reference of gestalt psychology remains as encapsulated within the organism as was that of classical psycho-physics.

Re behaviorism: Both peripheralism and physiologism in general demarcate the favorite regions of reference of the behaviorists with molecular leaning, that is, the organism as confined to its boundaries. . . . Hull's theory is entirely contained within the limits of the organism. . . . He is thus paying with molecular encapsulation for progress along nomothetic lines.

Re Cybernetics: While in the case of psychological functionalism the circular loop is apt to include smaller or larger portions of the surroundings before it boomerangs—mostly in a beneficial though sometimes in a harmful manner—, the feedback loops of computing machines are contained within the system itself. So far as this most intensively worked out core of the approach is concerned, Cybernetics corresponds to centralistic model-constructions with encapsulation within the organism. (**10**, pp. 70, 95, 122, 129)

In terms advanced by John Dewey and Bentley, we find in modern science a transition from self-actional to interactional and transactional conceptions. Classical neurophysiology and psychology are self-actional, i.e. take into account only linear causal trains. Gestalt theory is interactional, emphasizing dynamics within unified systems. The general trend of science, however, is directed towards transactional conceptions, namely, the organism in its environs. As was stated by Bentley (1), behavior and the relation between knowing and known can be considered as a special case of the wider conception of the organism as an open system.

SECOND ALTERNATIVE: MOLECULAR AND MOLAR MODELS

A second alternative may also be indicated in biological terms:

For understanding the phenomena of life . . . it is not only necessary to carry on analysis as far as possible, in order to know the individual components, but it is equally necessary to know the laws of order by which parts and partial processes are integrated, and which determine just the characteristic peculiarities of life. In the discovery of these system laws, the organismic conception sees the essential and specific object of biology. . . . Experience shows that precisely the "vital" characteristics proper seem to elude the usual (analytical) approach. . . . The processes in the living are so complicated that, *as far as the laws of organic systems as a whole are concerned*, we must reckon not with the individual physico-chemical processes, but with units of a biological order. . . . Biological laws, as in physiology of metabolism, in genetics, biocoenology, etc., represent "statistics of higher order" as compared to physics and chemistry. (**5**, pp. 31, 145-146, 161 ff.)

This corresponds to the antithesis of the so-called *molecular* and *molar* approach in psychology. We can either try an explanation by way of analysis into ever finer partial processes or try to establish global laws for phenomena as a whole. Functionalism emphasizes that only the latter approach leads to the essential problems and complies with the requirements of normalcy, naturalness, and "closeness to life."

A generalized statistical conception of psychology would serve to establish a unity of basic outlook and research design hitherto lacking within this discipline. . . . The fact that physics has better chances to find strict laws when becoming more macroscopic while psychology has better chances when becoming more microscopic, is not a paradox, however; macrophysics deals with phenomena of a grossly similar order of magnitude or coarseness as those of micro-psychology, while both above and below this stratum there is less stringent orderliness. (10, pp. 43, 47)

This corresponds to the biological maxims outlined above. It appears that the way to overcome the antithesis between analysis of isolated events and global laws, between molecular and molar approach, is to acknowledge the relative necessity of both ways:

There is a kind of complementarity between the analytical and the system conception. We can either isolate the individual processes in the organism and define them in physico-chemical terms, whereby, however, the whole eludes us owing to its tremendous complexity. Or we can state laws for the biological system as a whole, having to renounce, however, physico-chemical determination of the individual processes. (5, p. 146)

Third Alternative: Material and Formal Models

A third alternative can be termed as that of *material* and *formal model conceptions*. We can either build hypothetical constructs in the form of assumed entities; or we can try models that are noncommittal with respect to the entities concerned and only give a formalization of the laws of the phenomena under consideration. To the first type belong all interpretations in terms of hypothetical substances, structures, nerve connections, and the like. If such a hypothesis is correct, the entities assumed are later demonstrated in direct observation. The second way of approach is less evident though it is quite common in the evolution of science. For example, classical thermodynamics is a construct of the formal type, the notions of entropy, of the Carnot cycle, etc. being abstract and unvisualizable. Later, kinetic theory transformed thermodynamics into a theory of the material type, explaining, for example, entropy by the movement of molecules and their probable distributions. Similarly, Mendel's original system was a formal theory. It gave the laws of the distribution of hereditary characters in successive generations of hybrids, but Mendel knew nothing about chromosomes, meiosis, haploid and diploid cells and so forth, and the material basis of heredity was discovered much later.

History of science shows that constructs of the formal type are highly useful, especially in the earlier stages of scientific development. Later, material models can be established and verified in direct observation. Adhering to material models and trying to explain all phenomena in terms of hypothetical substances or structures appeals to the human preference for what can be visualized, touched, and analyzed. It may lead, however, to the hypostatization of structures where there are none because the order is essentially dynamic, to one-sided elementaristic conceptions, and to disregard, or shifting into metaphysics, of those problems which are not handy for material interpretation.

As far as psychology is concerned, little is known about the material counterpart of mental experience in the brain. So it may be useful, instead of elaborating hypothetical neural mechanisms, first to try a formalization of what seem to be the essential laws in this realm. This is in the spirit of American functionalism whose "ignoring of the brain" has been characterized as an approach which is "less physiological and more biological" (10, p. 107).

It may be that a general theory of systems which was developed by the present author (7) can serve as a starting point for such approach. In fact, those very concepts which are most basic for psychological theory, such as wholeness and summativity, progressive segregation, mechanization and centralization, leading parts, finality and equifinality, anamorphosis, and so on can be defined in General System Theory, and the theory is ready to be filled with the contents of neurological and psychological facts.

TOWARDS AN ORGANISMIC MODEL OF PERSONALITY

Thus it appears that model conceptions in psychological theory should be (a) essentially dynamic, although including structural order, established by progressive mechanization, as a derived yet most important case; (b) molar, though allowing for molecular interpretation of the individual processes; (c) formal, though allowing for future material interpretations.

In conclusion, a tentative definition of the living organism may be mentioned: A living organism is a hierarchy of open systems maintaining itself in a steady state due to its inherent system conditions (5, p. 124).

It appears that a corresponding definition could be applied as a general model of personality. The dynamic character of behavioral and psychological systems has already been discussed. The hierarchical organization of the processes in behavior is evident (5, p. 50). Hierarchical order similarly holds true in the architecture of personality where, roughly speaking, three levels are superimposed. The first is the spinal cord as a reflex apparatus; the second, the palaencephalon as the organ of the depth personality with its primeval instincts, emotions, and appetites; the third, piled on top of the latter, the cortex as the organ of the day personality of consciousness. Rothacker (22) has exposed the "stratification of personality," and it is easy to relate it to the strata of the central nervous system.

The universe of symbols created by man's day personality distinguishes him from all other beings (4). It replaces the corporeal trial and error, as it is found in lower organisms, by reasoning, i.e. trial and error in conceptual symbols. Phylogenetic evolution, based upon hereditary changes, is supplanted by history, based upon the tradition of symbols. Goal-seeking behavior is a general biological characteristic; true purposiveness is a privilege of man and is based upon the anticipation of the future in symbols. Instead of being a product, man becomes the creator of his environment. On the other hand, the antagonism between the levels of personality is at the bottom of the human tragedy. If there comes a clash between the world of symbols, built up as the moral values and concepts of humanity, and biological drives out of place in the environment of civilization, then, with respect to the individual, the situation of psychoneurosis arises. As a social factor that universe of symbols which is unique to man creates the sanguinary course of history. As opposed to the naïve struggle for existence in organisms, without malice and resulting from competition for food and for living space, history is determined by the struggle of ideologies—worlds of symbols, which is the more cruel the more they veil primitive instincts. Thus man has to pay for his uniqueness that elevates him above other beings. Whether the levels of personality can be properly adjusted is the question upon which man's future depends.

REFERENCES

1. BENTLEY, A. F. Kennetic inquiry. *Science*, 1950, 112, 775-783.
2. BERTALANFFY, L. VON. *Modern theories of development*. Trans. by J. H. Woodger. Oxford: Oxford Univ. Press, 1933.
3. BERTALANFFY, L. VON. *Das Gefuege des Lebens*. Leipzig: B. G. Teubner, 1937.
4. BERTALANFFY, L. VON. Das biologische Weltbild. *III. Internationale Hochschulwochen des Oesterr. College in Alpbach*, 1948, 251-274.
5. BERTALANFFY, L. VON. *Das biologische Weltbild*. Bern: A. Franke, 1949. Trans.: *Problems of life: an evaluation of modern biological thought*. London: Watts & Co. (In press.)
6. BERTALANFFY, L. VON. The theory of open systems in physics and biology. *Science*, 1950, 111, 23-29.
7. BERTALANFFY, L. VON. An outline of general system theory. *Brit. J. Philos. Sci.*, 1950, 1, 134-165.
8. BETHE, A. Plastizitaet und Zentrenlehre. *Handb. norm. u. pathol. Physiol.*, 1931, 15/2.
9. BETHE, A., AND FISCHER, E. Anpassungsfaehigkeit (Plastizitaet) des Nervensystems. *Handb. norm. u. pathol. Physiol.*, 1931, 15/2.
10. BRUNSWIK, E. *The conceptual framework of psychology*. Internat. Encyclopedia of Unified Science. Vol. I, No. 10. Chicago: Univ. of Chicago Press, 1950. (Preliminary mimeographed edition.)
11. CANTRIL, H., et al. Psychology and scientific research. *Science*, 1949, 110, 461-464, 491-497, 517-522.
12. GOLDSTEIN, K. *The organism*. New York: American Book Co., 1939.
13. HOLST, E. VON. Von der Mathematik der nervoesen Ordnungsfunktion. *Experientia*, 1948, 4, 374-381.
14. KRECH, D. Dynamic systems as open neurological systems. *Psychol. Rev.*, 1950, 57, 345-361.
15. KRECHEVSKY, I. Brain mechanisms and variability. *J. comp. Psychol.*, 1937, 23, 121-138.
16. KRUEGER, F. *Lehre vom Ganzen*. Beiheft z. Schweiz. Z. f. Psychol., No. 15. Bern: Hans Huber, 1948.
17. LASHLEY, K. S. *Brain mechanisms and intelligence*. Chicago: Univ. of Chicago Press, 1929.
18. LORENZ, K. Der Kumpan in der Umwelt des Vogels. *J. Ornithol.*, 1935, 83.
19. RASHEVSKY, N. Learning a property of physical systems. Brain mechanisms and their physical models. *J. gen. Psychol.*, 1931, 5.
20. RASHEVSKY, N. *Mathematical biophysics* (2nd Ed.). Chicago: Univ. of Chicago Press, 1948.
21. ROHRACHER, H. *Lehrbuch der Psychologie* (2nd Ed.). Wien: Urban & Schwarzenberg, 1948.
22. ROTHACKER, E. *Die Schichten der Persoenlichkeit* (3rd Ed.). Leipzig: J. A. Barth, 1947.
23. WIENER, N. *Cybernetics*. New York: J. Wiley, 1948.

The Role of Neurological Ideas in Psychology

D. O. HEBB
McGill University

T HIS is partly a public profession of faith (although, to paraphrase W. H. Fowler, the writer's opinions have already been allowed to appear with indecent plainness elsewhere). It is my conviction that we have no choice but to physiologize in psychology, overtly or covertly. Tolman (26) has said that conscious theory is better than unconscious, even if bad. As the author of a bad theory, in what I conceive to be Tolman's sense, I am in an excellent position to spell out his point. But—a warning to the reader—this is not modesty. My argument is that it is only with the rubble of bad theories that we shall be able to build better ones, and that without theory of some kind, somewhere, psychological observation and description would at best be chaotic and meaningless.

There is not space here to develop any neurologically biased treatment of personality. This task must be left for other papers, including the results of some animal experiments now going on (1). What we shall be concerned with here is the rationale of the neurological model in psychological theory,[1] including the theory of personality.

PHYSIOLOGY NO SIN WHEN PUBLICLY RECOGNIZED

Christian thought has always held that sexual congress is inherently sinful, but man is frail. The church therefore has realistically provided for biological facts in the solemn rite of marriage while still stoutly opposing any illicit, unblessed, transient, or haphazard union that has not had formal public approval. Matrimony removes the stigma. More, it makes the family possible; so one can even argue that the openly recognized sexual union has positive virtues.

---

[1] On attempting to review the literature, I find that I cannot begin to acknowledge aid from all the various sources that have influenced this discussion, but I do wish to cite English (5), Geldard (6), Pratt (20), Köhler (11), and Loucks (15) in addition to those referred to in the text.

For all this there is a parallel in the dealings of psychology with physiology. Here too there are biological facts that cannot be overlooked, and there is the same superiority of a recognized liaison over furtive ones. Let me try to justify such ideas.

For twenty years or so there has been a vigorous attempt in psychology (and psychiatry) to be rid of "physiologizing" or "neurologizing." It has been said that physiological concepts are too limited, restrict theory too much. Krech (13) has argued that instead of turning away from a narrow physiology (narrow presumably because incomplete), we must expand neurological and physiological conceptions to meet the psychological facts. This is sound enough, although I shall try to show later that there are in practice limits to such a theoretical procedure. By using exactly the procedure that Krech advocates, psychology has repeatedly anticipated neurophysiology, the purely behavioral evidence indicating the existence of neural processes not known at the time but discovered independently by the physiologist later.

But one must seriously doubt that it was the narrowness of physiological conceptions that made them unpopular with psychologists. With some men, yes, but not with others, because the antiphysiological point of view shows no positive correlation with the breadth and flexibility of the theory that has resulted in each case.

Those who renounced the shackles of neurology did not, in general, go on unshackled to develop a richer and fuller account of behavior. Some of them retreated instead into the chains of an earlier and still less enlightened neurology, dated 1890 instead of 1930 or '40. This particular group can be discussed first, leaving others like Tolman to a later section.

The idea in rejecting physiology was to use only "purely behavioral" conceptions, but some of these were actually of physiological origin and continue to exert a physiological influence on psychology. The influence is evident in several ways, but most convincingly I think in certain omissions that can be traced back to Sherrington, Waldeyer, and Cajal: to the neuron theory and the irreversibility of conduction at the synapse (without the significant qualification of such ideas that has been made since 1930 or thereabouts by electrophysiology). Murphy (19, pp. 188-189) has noted how great an effect the neuron-synapse conception had. The effect was of two kinds. Primarily, in my opinion, it was clarifying and stimulating; but it was also negative, leading to the exclusion of ideas that otherwise could have remained in psychological theory. Among them one can list (a) association between sensory processes (as distinct from sensori-motor association), and (b) ideation, imagery, and related notions. In 1890, an association of one sensory event with another (or of one image with another) was not only an acceptable notion, it was the cement that held psychological theory together. By 1920 such association was doubtful at best, and so was the mere existence of ideas, or of anything central but one-way connections running from receptor to effector. Why? Not on psychological grounds, surely—psychologically, the existence of images and sensory associations is hard to deny; even in a completely objective psychology there are observations of animal or man that would be much easier to account for by postulating such things. But in that thirty-year interval between 1890 and 1920, a valuable neurological hypothesis had been developed which had plenty of room for S-R connections and motor thought, but none for S-S connections or "autonomous" central processes (i.e., ones that do not depend moment by moment on any particular sensory stimulation). It should be clear that this was not a bad development for theory. The increased precision of ideas and better formulation of problems far outweighed a temporary loss of breadth. The point here is that the exclusion of S-S connections and ideation was of physiological origin.

Any later theory that continues the exclusion is permitting the faulty neurophysiology of 1920 (at the latest) to determine its main outlines. If we must be influenced by ideas about how the nervous system works, those of the 1940 variety make it possible to regain some of James's breadth without losing the benefits gained from Cajal and Sherrington and built into psychological theory by the litigation of Hobhouse vs. Thorndike and Lashley vs. Pavlov. I do not suggest any subordination of psychology to physiology, but only that psychology must be influenced by physiological evidence, as neurophysiology is influenced by psychological evidence. It is clear that the psychologist's first concern is the behavior of the normal, intact animal, and theory must not do violence to the facts of behavior (though it may be very difficult sometimes to show that violence has been done—that is, to refute a theory decisively by behavioral evidence). But though behavioral evidence is not inferior to anatomical and physiological evidence, neither is it superior.

Again, the conception of mental set or of attention as a causal agent in perception (instead of a by-product)—how are we to understand the absence of this from a "pure" psychology, except by the fact that it is inconsistent with the 1920 conception of the nervous system as a collection of through routes, one-way streets, from sense organ to muscle or gland? Why has there been such a profound reluctance (7) to postulate something going on within the animal that opens the door to one kind of stimulation and closes it to another? There is plenty of factual evidence that this sort of thing happens all the time in behavior, and plenty of physical models to suggest how, conceivably, it might come about. There is the modern dial telephone's selector switch, for example, or the catalyst idea from chemistry, or the joint action of dust and water vapor to form fog or rain. It is not mysterious therefore to postulate attention as something that acts as co-chairman in charge of response, jointly with the present stimulus itself. Not mysterious, that is, unless one's thinking is controlled unwittingly by the picture of a nervous system in which such things are impossible.

It thus appears that S-R theory is not merely physiological in descent or in its Pavlovian terminology, but by its persistent exclusion of psychologically justified conceptions it also shows that it is still essentially physiological. Failing to recognize this it to disregard one source of error. If we must be chained to physiological ideas, we should at least choose the modern ones that allow more freedom of movement.

In short, let us espouse our physiology openly so that we know which member of the family it is that we are sleeping with and especially so that we can avoid the one who, charming and mature as she was in 1920, is less satisfying now, not to say less fertile.

TOLMAN, PHENOMENOLOGY, AND THE NEED OF THEORY

So much for the influence of neurology and physiology as exerted through the stimulus-response idea. Does the psychologist who rejects S-R theory thereby avoid the influence?

No one I believe has been as successful as Tolman in giving a systematic but nonphysiological account of behavior (assuming that Hull's is physiological). At the same time, I think it is clear (a) that his starting point was Holt's or Watson's scheme of the nervous system together with the destructive effect on it of Lashley's extirpation experiments, and (b) that the subsequent course of his work shows how short the tether is on which explanation can stray from its physiological origins.

What Tolman did essentially was to have responses initiated by stimulus patterns instead of stimuli, and to replace the ideation that Thorndike had thrown out. He also included a postulate of attention, in his "means-end-readiness," which psychology clearly needed but which no one else had the stomach for. But this effort, while it represents both imagination and courage, is by no means a holus-bolus rejection of Watson and the earlier Thorndike or of the products of their physiologizing. By not making a neural hypothesis explicit, Tolman *may* have been freer to postulate things that are not immediately reduceable to neural terms, but this is doubtful. The same kind of thing is done in another way: "There is a neural process X with such-and-such behavioral manifestations, whose exact mechanism and locus cannot be specified for the moment, but which the behavioral evidence requires." This is what Krech has said the psychologist must do to broaden neurological theory for his own purposes, and it has been historically an important part of the psychological method. Tolman might have neurologized and still been free to recognize the facts of behavior.

The absence of neurological terms in Tolman's writing does not per se mean any real discontinuity with the physiological thinking of Holt and Watson, nor for that matter with the equally physiological thought of the Gestalt group. What Tolman offered was a modification and synthesis of these two superficially incompatible approaches, both of which were affected in their main outlines by ideas of neural function. He did not start with a clean slate, and to suppose that he did, that he could really ·have freed himself from the influence of earlier physiologizing, is to forget how short the steps are in the growth of theory.

Furthermore, the extent to which Tolman and his students have been negative and defensive in their later work in the latent-learning argument, looking for phenomena that their opponents could not explain more than developing their own theoretical structure, demonstrates the trouble that theory has had in getting far from the physiologically intelligible. Tolman's group have apparently felt a continuous pressure to show that ideation is still a necessary conception. The reason seems to be that the charge of mysticism and an unscientific vagueness has always hung over their heads. It could not have done so if they had turned to a modern neurophysiology and shown that it makes ideation, in a crude way at least, necessary as well as intelligible. The question of ideation at bottom is the question of whether central neural processes .go on in the absence of an adequate sensory arousal, and all modern electrophysiology indicates that the activity of the brain is continuous and that the effect of a sensory event is not to arouse inactive tissue but to modify the activity already going on. Denny-Brown (4) made a similar point about set or attention: the effect of a sensory event upon motor behavior must always be subject to modification by the pre-existent activity of the brain. In other words, the work of Berger, Adrian, Lorento de Nó, and Morison and Dempsey could have been a safe-conduct to free Tolman from the necessity of continual defense—even defense in the form of attack—and to allow him to develop his own ideas further.

It has been suggested that physiology "cannot cast any vote" in the choice of psychological principles. Whether it should or not, it always has. It is now clear that Wertheimer and Köhler were on the right track about 1920 in their account of the afferent visual process, well in advance of the neurologist. Essentially, they were postulating an interaction among cells at the same level in transmission from the retina. If one will read for example Marshall and Talbot (17), one will find a very Gestalt-like account of activity in area seventeen of the cortex, based on physiological knowledge derived mostly after 1930. But despite the actual soundness of the Gestalt position, both psychologically and neurologically, it was vehemently rejected as mystical because it was "known" in 1920 that the nervous system does not act in that way.

Was such a vote (in this case, a wrong one) possible only in the neurologically deluded twenties? Not at all. Spence's brilliant treatment of insight and the sudden solution in discrimination learning (24, 25) had a profound effect on those "tough-minded" psychologists who were (and are) opposed to physiologizing. For them, to judge from the literature, the evidence of insight reported by Köhler (10) and Krech (12) was not so until Spence showed how it might be dealt with. But Spence's solution could be tough-minded (i.e., provide an intelligible mechanism of response) because the conception of physiological gradients was already familiar from embryological studies; familiarized in biology by Kappers and Child (it is credited to them by Lashley (14), who also used the idea theoretically), it was used as well in a frankly physiological sense by Pavlov and the Gestalt group. Spence had a physiological passport even while he denied physiologizing.

A final and extreme example of the present day: why do we not accept ESP as a psychological fact? Rhine has offered enough evidence to have convinced us on almost any other issue where one could make some guess as to the mechanics of the disputed process. Some of his evidence has been explained away, but as far as I can find out, not all of it. Until a complete rebuttal is provided or until we accept ESP, let us not talk about enlarging our notions of neurology to meet the psychological "facts" with no external criterion of what those facts are. We are still trying to find our way out of the magic wood of animism, where psychology began historically, and we cannot give up the talisman of a knowledge of material processes. Personally, I do not accept ESP for a moment, because it does not make sense. My external criteria, both of physics and of physiology, say that ESP is not a fact despite the behavioral evidence that has been reported. I cannot see what other basis my colleagues have for rejecting it; and if they are using my basis, they and I are allowing psychological evidence to be passed on by physical and physiological censors. Rhine may still turn out to be right, improbable as I think that is, and my own rejection of his views is—in the literal sense—prejudice.

The theory of behavior must ultimately be consistent with both behavioral and physiological evidence. Either discipline can black-ball the idea that strays too far from existing knowledge, even conceivably the sound idea that it should not. If some ultra-genius, with divine revelation, suddenly turned up one day with a "true" and complete theory of behavior as it may ultimately be known some millennia from now, he might find it impossible even to get a hearing from psychologists for what would seem preposterously unreal notions. The situation would be like one in which Einstein on being admitted to the houseboat on the Styx tried to explain quantum mechanics to Archimedes and Euclid, these persons not having yet heard of the electron, of the way in which electromagnetic waves can exist in a nonexistent ether, or even of the theory of gravitation. We commonly think of a theory as right or wrong, true or untrue: but is there any possibility at all of having a true theory of behavior today? Newton was a genius because his theories could be accepted for 250 years or so, but they are not thought to be correct or adequate today. The best we can ask therefore is that a theory should be good, not correct.

And in psychology we must expect to have to work our way progressively through a series of ideas, of better and better theories. It is not by any means a condemnation of S-R theory to say that it is narrow or that there are facts which (we are now pretty sure) it cannot comprehend. The significant question is not whether Thorndike's account of animal learning was right, but whether it helped us to see better the problems involved and led to new analyses. In Hull's systematizing, in Tolman's ability to define purpose without philosophic teleology, in Lashley's analysis of animal perception, or Köhler's and Krech's experimental demonstrations of insight, the evidence is clear concerning the stimulating and clarifying value of stimulus-response theory and its erroneous (because incomplete) physiological foundation.

This point of view shows how to clear up a possible ambiguity in the discussion by MacLeod (16) and Smith (23) concerning the way in which a phenomenologist goes about his business. The suggestion is that the phenomenologist is one who puts aside bias (either of theory or of common sense) and simply observes what is before him. But MacLeod then adds that this is never entirely possible and speaks of observing with a "disciplined naïveté." The ambiguity comes in the possible interpretation that getting rid of theory completely would make for the clearest observation (or in the apparent contradiction of discipline and naïveté). From the point of view we have now arrived at, an answer is possible for this difficulty. It is not getting rid of theory entirely that is needed (otherwise the thing to do would be to get a backwoodsman, or someone else who had never heard of psychology, to observe in one's experiments), but to put theory in the background instead of the foreground where it blocks one's vision. The "discipline" is in a thorough knowledge of theory; the "naïveté" consists of trying to find other ways of looking at the world besides the one dictated by existing theory. Essentially, phenomenology means looking for new biases, not getting rid of bias.

I have spoken of the common observation that theory moves by short steps. This observation may be thought of as implying only a negative influence from earlier theory, as providing evidence simply of the inertia of human thought. But there must be more to the process than that. Einstein's formulation would not have been possible without the observations gathered under the influence of Newton's ideas. Earlier theories, then, are limiting for a very good reason. They are what one climbs on to get to the next stage —it is also a common observation that a stepladder is *very* narrow and limiting, when one is using it.

In other words, we must recognize the positive value even of "wrong" theories as guides to observation. If the phenomenologist could really divest himself of all his theoretical knowledge and tried then to record the facts of his own perception or of an animal's behavior, what would he choose to put down on paper? There are an infinite number of relationships and aspects of behavior, an infinitude of possible subdivisions of animal activity or of human thought. *Some* theoretical guide is necessary as a principle of selection.

What the phenomenologically minded individual has always recorded is what he sees that is related to, but inconsistent with, existing theory. It is in such a sense only that he avoids bias, and this of course is not really avoiding it. A better way of defining a phenomenologist might be to say that he is one of those who, at the extreme, do not like existing theories (and perhaps never will) but are interested in attacking them and finding evidence that is hard for theory to handle: an "agin-the-established-order" attitude, anti-theoretical but not a-theoretical, which historically has been an important source of new ideas and experiments.

A figure of speech used elsewhere may help to clear this up. There appears to be a left wing and a right wing in psychology, paralleling Left and Right in politics, and the activity of the Left cannot be understood if one does not see that the only continuity in its behavior is in being against the Right. In psychology the Right favors parsimony of explanatory ideas, a simple or mechanical account of behavior, and definiteness even at the cost of being narrow. The Left is prepared to postulate more freely and can better tolerate vagueness and a lack of system in its account of behavior. Thus Gestalt psychology, especially in its early years, could develop a theory of perception and a theory of thought that were not brought into any clear relationship with one another, and a theory of memory ("traces") that seemed downright inconsistent with the Gestalt account of perception. But the primary motivation was not to develop a theory; it was to demonstrate the shortcomings of stimulus-response theory, and the scientific benefits that accrued from this effort are obvious—just as obvious as the fact that such an attitude (which includes the phenomenologist's) is not possible without a theory to attack.

THE BACONIAN FALLACY

The idea that one could observe more clearly if one could divest himself of all preceding theory, or that psychology would be better off without theory, is related to a widespread epistemological misconception concerning the scientific method. This notion goes back through J. S. Mill to Francis Bacon and can, for convenience here, be called the Baconian fallacy. It is in the first place the idea that scientific generalizations are arrived at by "induction," by counting noses, and from this derives the idea that scientific laws are empirical. It implies that there are a limited number of "facts," "events," or properties of any object or situation, so that the scientist can proceed by simply describing, even, if it is desirable, by recording *everything* that happens in conjunction with whatever phenomenon he is interested in. There is no useful purpose for creative imagination. Causes can be discovered simply by assiduity: list everything that preceded the to-be-explained event, on a thousand or ten thousand occasions if necessary, and if your lists are complete, the cause will be the one thing that is on every list. (In practice there are short cuts, and the lists may be remembered instead of written out.)

But anyone can see that there is something wrong here when the crude implications of the induction idea are followed up in this way. The next step is to abandon an interest in causes (especially hypothetical causes that can hardly get into one's lists) and at a high level of sophistication regard scientific law as a statement of probability only, and science as description. Theory is tautology and self-delusion.

To such views the following propositions may be opposed.

(A) Induction and counting cases are only methods of demonstration or of testing a generalization already arrived at (often on the basis of a single case).

(B) The typical scientific law is not a summary of observations and has nothing to do with probability but is a working postulate or mode of thought. If apparent contradictions of a useful law are observed, one promptly postulates something else to account for them instead of discarding the law.

(C) Of such modes of thought, the cause-and-effect one is still generally used though not a necessary way of thinking nor valuable in all situations.

(D) The scientist is characteristically concerned with his postulated entities more than with the phenomena they were inferred from (the chemist interested in atomic weights rather than in weights of actual materials, the physicist interested in neutrons and mesons rather than photographs of cloud chambers or even bombs). Science itself is characteristically an elaborate structure of imagined entities and events.

(E) Since there is an infinity of things that can be recorded in any situation, a complete description is a meaningless conception along with a purely descriptive science. Constructs may be formally tautological and yet have the practical function of guiding observation.

These propositions may be clearer with a few examples. Newton's first law of motion has been a profoundly valuable theoretical tool, but it certainly was not an induction or summary description, for no such event as an object's continuing to move indefinitely with uniform speed in a straight line has ever been observed—not even once, nor an approximation thereto. To make the law a statement of probability is nonsense. One can assume that it is true, or that it is not true; and one can then go on to see what other assumptions must also be made and what deductions can be made from them. Experimental verification amounts to showing that the whole set is consistent with facts or leads to the discovery of new facts, also consistent.

The law of gravitation *is* a vast and impressive tautology:

forces are mythical, and postulating a force of gravitation that is known only through the phenomena it is supposed to explain really adds nothing to the facts—not in this sense. But if we think of the construct of gravity as a statement of a new way of thinking, which made the tide, the orbit of the earth, and falling downstairs all examples of a single class of phenomena, one can see better the practical role of even a tautological construct. Reclassifying a group of facts does not add to the number of facts classified, but the reclassification is a significant fact itself. Logically, perhaps explanation reduces to ordering and classifying phenomena only, but it is impossible for man to think consistently in such terms.

The atom and the electron are just as much constructs as gravity, for no one has ever seen or handled either though it is now hard to realize that they are not facts (i.e., directly known phenomena). Their function too must be heuristic, as long as one is being utterly logical. It is perhaps a weakness of the human intellect that it must resort to such devices, but I think it is clear that thought is incorrigible in this respect. Thinking does not proceed according to formal logic, even in natural science or mathematics (Courant and Robbins [3], Conant [2], Hadamard [8]) and attempting to act as if it did must be sterile.

If, as it seems, the scientist inveterately resorts to imagined things and properties of things to fill in the gaps as it were in natural phenomena, his problem is to imagine the right things, to choose the constructs that do increase order in perceived events (or make possible an orderly universe that is more imagined than perceived). Sometimes the clarifying effect of a newly postulated entity is so immediate and extensive that its value is obvious. It is a "discovery," at once accepted as "true." But often, because one is dealing with a number of postulates at once, so that the same effect might perhaps be achieved by changing some other postulate, the fruitfulness of the new conception is not clear at once, and often it is only an approximation to the fruitful one. At this stage in investigation the philosophically naïve scientist merely asks of his hunch, "Is it so?" and tries to test its reality in every way he can. He does not stay at the level of his original observations but applies any test he can think of. Such an idea of reality may be an innocent one, but it makes for scientific results. Perhaps we should describe the process of testing the value of a construct in other terms; but we cannot afford to omit it. In psychology the intervening variables, we know, are actually neural and physiological; the refusal to neurologize amounts to discarding a guide to the selection of one's constructs. It is refusing to look at data that might show that one's theory is wrong.

If only because of the frailty of man's intellect, we must theorize. In theorizing, we cannot afford to neglect any available information, so that theory must be consonant with knowledge of the nervous system although, if one wishes, one can choose terms that conceal the fact. Skinner (22) is the one, of course, whose effective experimental work may make the strongest argument against such conclusions. But I believe that it is only Skinner's high personal level of ability, in despite of an erroneous epistemology, that has made these successes possible. Even he slips into the use of constructs occasionally (e.g., in the "reflex reserve"), and he may be much more dependent on earlier neurologizing than he thinks, as I have argued above of Spence and Tolman. If all theoretical systems of behavior were really forgotten, not even Skinner could continue with simple description.

THE NERVOUS SYSTEM AND PERSONALITY

And now finally for the specific relevance of neurology to the theory of personality. In such a discussion as this the proof of the pudding is in the eating, and my argument may ultimately stand or fall with the usefulness of my own neurologically related theory (9) or the better theory it helps to engender.

The S-R model did not really offer a very good framework for the theory of personality, and even Mowrer (18), ingenious and stimulating as he is, shows signs of strain in trying to make it serve such a purpose. In earlier days, before the elaborate structure of "secondary reinforcement" had been developed to allow one to have the law of effect without its consequences, it is probable that not even a beginning at a rapprochement between S-R-neurological theory and personality would have been possible. Freud and Lewin very likely were wise to choose other models.

My argument has not been that a neurologically based model is essential to psychological thought (all the literary insights based on the common-sense, animistic model of "mind" bear witness to the contrary). The argument is (a) that some scheme or model is necessary in practice, if not logically; (b) that the S-R model has served well and (with alterations) is the base of further theorizing; and (c) that psychology eventually will be using a "real" neurological model. Freud's schematizing would have been severely cramped, at the very least, by any effort to stick to the then available neurological conceptions. On the other hand, the models of both Freud and Lewin have serious defects as well as advantages; and when neurologically based theory can be enlarged to fit in the Freudian and Lewinian ideas, modified as necessary, our understanding both of personality and of apparently less complex phenomena should be greatly increased.

It is important however to say that there is no question of attempting to translate complex human processes directly into terms of neuron and synapse. At the very least there must intervene hypothetical "central motive states," "dynamic systems," "symbolic processes," or "phase cycles." The number of functional relations between the single cells in Mr. Doe's brain, determining his behavior, is for practical purposes infinite. Even if we put aside the things men have in common and try only to record the connections that are different from those in Mr. Roe's brain, the number must still be impossibly large. We need grosser units of analysis. What shall they be?

For the present they must be at the level of such familiar working conceptions as irritability, self-confidence, attitudes toward society, and so on and so forth: the rough sort of psychological analysis of personality that we now make. Further, the analysis in my judgment will always be in psychological terms. They will not be our present terms, and they may have explicit physiological reference (as "stimulus" and "reflex" have) but nonetheless will be ones which have been developed by psychologists to deal with a psychological problem.

The study of behavior requires co-operative analysis at a number of levels at once. This process implies a series of reductions, from the level of personality study to phenomena of isolated nerve fibers. Since "reductionism" seems well on its way to becoming a new term of abuse (like "molecular") I should like to be more explicit here.

The student of social psychology for example tries to understand crowd behavior by analyzing it, or reducing it, to the behavior of a number of individuals, which indeed it is. However, he finds at once the interesting thing about crowds, that they do not act as one would predict from what we know about the individual members of the crowd, at the present state of knowledge. The whole seems quite different from the sum of its parts; that is, it shows that the parts have properties that were not detected in isolation. The analysis is unsuccessful in a sense, but making it, and finding it unsatisfactory, tells one more about the crowd and the individuals therein. Similarly, the student of spinal-cord function tries to reduce it to a collection of independent reflexes, and the failure to make this work means a better understanding of the individual reflex and of reflex integration.

First, analysis, real or hypothetical; then synthesis, putting the parts back together again to see what was lost or distorted in the analysis—which is one's guide to a better analysis next time. Understanding a complex process means nothing else than that one can make the hypothetical analysis without loss or distortion. We do not yet fully understand behavior, which is to say that our present analytical conceptions are unsatisfactory and that we must look for better ones. It is not the attempt to analyze that is bad, but the being content with a poor analysis.

Thus the social psychologist is continually pressing for better conceptions from the student of emotion, of perception, of learning, and so forth. But the student of emotion (is it necessary to say that this may actually be the same person working at another level because no one else is interested in making the experiments he wants done?)—the student of emotion has in turn a similar relation to the student of conditioning, or of sensory mechanisms, or of the anatomy of the hypothalamus. The thinker in each area is guided by those around him, provided he can use their language. It is not necessary that the student of personality talk in neurological terms, but his terms should be translatable when necessary into neurology. Physiologizing is not a substitute for psychology but an aid to it.

The theory that I have proposed (9) is primarily a psychological one, not neurological. Its main outlines are determined by an effort to comprehend certain behavioral facts. If it were really a neurological (rather than neurologically oriented) one, it would be concerned mainly with anatomical and electrophysiological data and only extended into the behavioral realm as far as solid neurological warrant is available (which is not very far). If my presentation is examined, however, one will find that the solid neurological warrant is frequently missing—as the critics have noted, my explanations are vague or incomplete in places, and there is a considerable use of neurological assumption. The theory really operates at a number of levels at once, the neurologizing consisting of a search for liaison of (a) psychological construct with (b) anatomical and physiological fact, to the extent that the facts are available.

But it is also significant, I believe, that this search for liaison, the attempt to stick as far as possible to the physiologically intelligible, produced a broadening of the psychological horizon. The conceptions developed to deal with a very restricted set of problems (retention of ability after brain operation) opened my eyes to the significance of von Senden's (21) data on vision after congenital cataract, for example; provided for the first time a conceptual frame into which the variable causes and forms of emotion would fit; and led from there to a more inclusive account of human motivation. The apparent necessity of assuming two stages of learning, on purely neurological grounds, at once drew attention to a number of commonly known facts of child development that have not been comprehended by theory. And so on. Though the theory must be wrong in detail throughout, the way in which it repeatedly drew attention to behavioral relationships not noted before, or rearranged the evidence more meaningfully, gives some basis for feeling that the general line it follows may be the direction that future theory will take. Physiologizing need not be limiting and narrow in its psychological effects but may actually broaden.

To return to an earlier figure of speech, the moral is that an interest in neural anatomy and physiology may make more work for the midwife of psychological ideas than for the undertaker.

REFERENCES

1. CLARKE, R. S., HERON, W., FETHERSTONHAUGH, M. L., FORGAYS, D. G., AND HEBB, D. O. Individual differences in dogs: preliminary report on the effects of early experience. *Canad. J. Psychol.*, 1951, **5**, No. 4.

2. CONANT, J. B. *On understanding science.* New Haven: Yale Univ. Press, 1947.

3. COURANT, R., AND ROBBINS, H. *What is mathematics?* London: Oxford Univ. Press, 1941.

4. DENNY-BROWN, D. Theoretical deductions from the physiology of the cerebral cortex. *J. Neurol. Psychopath.*, 1932, **13**, 52-67.

5. ENGLISH, H. B. The ghostly tradition and the descriptive categories of psychology. *Psychol. Rev.*, 1933, **40**, 498-513.

6. GELDARD, F. A. "Explanatory principles" in psychology. *Psychol Rev.*, 1939, **46**, 411-424.

7. GIBSON, J. J. A critical review of the concept of set in contemporary experimental psychology. *Psychol. Bull.*, 1941, **38**, 781-817.

8. HADAMARD, J. *The psychology of invention in the mathematical field.* Princeton: Princeton Univ. Press, 1945.

9. HEBB, D. O. *The organization of behavior: a neuropsychological theory.* New York: Wiley, 1949.

10. KÖHLER, W. *The mentality of apes.* New York: Harcourt, Brace, 1925.

11. KÖHLER, W. *Dynamics in psychology.* New York: Liveright, 1940.

12. KRECH, D. "Hypotheses" versus "chance" in the pre-solution period in sensory discrimination-learning. *Univ. Calif. Publ. Psychol.*, 1932, **6**, 27-44.

13. KRECH, D. Dynamic systems, psychological fields, and hypothetical constructs. *Psychol. Rev.*, 1950, **57**, 283-290.

14. LASHLEY, K. S. *Brain mechanism and intelligence.* Chicago: Univ. of Chicago Press, 1929.

15. LOUCKS, R. B. The contribution of physiological psychology. *Psychol. Rev.*, 1941, **48**, 105-126.

16. MACLEOD, R. B. The phenomenological approach to social psychology. *Psychol. Rev.*, 1947, **54**, 193-210.

17. MARSHALL, W. H., AND TALBOT, S. A. Recent evidence for neural mechanisms in vision leading to a general theory of sensory acuity. *Biol. Symp.*, 1942, **7**, 117-164.

18. MOWRER, O. H. *Learning theory and personality dynamics: selected papers.* New York: Ronald, 1950.

19. MURPHY, G. *Historical introduction to modern psychology* (2nd Ed.). New York: Harcourt, Brace, 1949.

20. PRATT, C. C. *The logic of modern psychology.* New York: Macmillan, 1939.

21. SENDEN, M. v. *Raum- und Gestaltauffassung bei Operierten Blindgeborenen vor und nach der Operation.* Leipzig: Barth, 1932.

22. SKINNER, B. F. *The behavior of organisms.* New York: Appleton Century, 1938.

23. SMITH, M. B. The phenomenological approach in personality theory: some critical remarks. *J. abnorm. soc. Psychol.*, 1950, **45**, 516-522.

24. SPENCE, K. W. Gradual versus sudden solution of discrimination problems by chimpanzees. *J. comp. Psychol.*, 1938, **25**, 213-224.

25. SPENCE, K. W. Continuous versus noncontinuous interpretations of discrimination learning. *Psychol. Rev.*, 1940, **47**, 271-288.

26. TOLMAN, E. C. Discussion. *J. Personal.*, 1949, **18**, 48-50.

The Conceptual Model of Psychoanalysis

DAVID RAPAPORT
Riggs Foundation, Stockbridge, Mass.

FAVORING A PURELY PSYCHOLOGICAL MODEL

I AM NOT EMBARKING on the task of creating a new model, but only of spelling out the psychoanalytic one, which to my knowledge has never been explicitly done. Nevertheless, I feel obliged to state my belief as to its position in relation to other models.

The psychoanalytic model is a purely psychological one, yet to my mind is sufficiently flexible to meet the requirements others were created to meet. I should not like to be misunderstood on this point. I am not implying that psychoanalysis has the answers to all psychological questions, nor that its answers to the questions it has tackled so far are necessarily correct, nor that it has no limitations in regard to quantitative treatment. I am asserting only that the conceptual model implicit to psychoanalysis is sufficiently broad and flexible to embrace on the one hand those realms of psychological phenomena which other models effectively conceptualize, and on the other those realms which have remained intractable to them.

This I realize is a grandiloquent claim, and I do not expect to substantiate it in this presentation; the purpose is to call the reader's attention to the fact that the model to be presented has such a claim. I am not the first to advance it: Hartmann (13) and others (33) have stated it more explicitly than they have the model itself.

The only point which I wish to discuss in this connection is the purely psychological character of the model to be presented, since recently Tolman (39), Hebb (16), and Krech (18) have gone to bat for neural models and against purely psychological ones.

It is becoming the vogue to invoke physicists in discussing conceptual models for psychology. They are invoked on "open systems," on "feed-back" mechanisms, but rarely on their attempts to deal with biological issues.

Recently several physicists [e.g., Schroedinger (37) and Delbrueck (6)] have concerned themselves with biology. They have pointed out that biological events, unlike those of physics, are time-bound and historical and therefore cannot be treated with the usual methods of physics. They have concluded that the study of biological phenomena may necessitate new physical concepts. Delbrueck has suggested that to account for the biological realm of observations we may have to sacrifice our demand for description in quantum theoretical terms, just as in accounting for the behavior of the atom we had to sacrifice our demand for exact determination of the locus and/or momentum of the individual electron. They have stressed that biological phenomena can be expressed—and already have been, as in genetics—by valid biological laws despite our ignorance of the underlying and mediating physicochemical processes. Actually, these views expressed by physicists are quite like the arguments of molar behaviorists, and seem to hold for psychology also.

Putting it more directly, I feel that psychological observations should be integrated on their own terms and by constructs built on the basis of psychological models. Whether the results so reached can or cannot be directly related to a neural substratum is an important question, and as such, a subject matter for empirical exploration. But first a theory which embraces the psychological observations on hand must be evolved, and so far no model has provided a conceptual framework which does not disregard many areas of existing observation.

Concerning the Psychoanalytic Model

The psychoanalytic model is intended to account both for those processes characteristic of the developing individual, and those characteristic of the mature one. Therefore it is easiest presented dichotomously: first the primary model, and then the secondary model, which—so to speak—arises from it. The dichotomy is a matter of presentation, and the transition between the processes each half describes is fluid. The primary model is as necessary to account for many normal and pathological processes in the adult (dreams, illusions, hallucinations) as for the processes of early psychological development. Actually, it could be said that the primary model is merely an abortive form of the secondary one, and the two are an indivisible unity, linking together phenomena qualitatively as diverse as infantile rage and intentional, value-regulated, goal-seeking adult behavior.

The psychoanalytic model is intended to account for all the phenomena traditionally categorized trichotomously under the headings conation, cognition, affection. This model considers the phenomena so segregated to be merely aspects of a unitary process. Available language and custom make it convenient to use this terminology, and in so far as it is used here it is meant to refer not to three kinds of processes, but to aspects of a unitary process. This is particularly important since it will be convenient to discuss the psychoanalytic model in terms of this trichotomy, and if the unity here suggested is not kept in mind the impression may be that the conative model is the basic one, with the cognitive and affective ones only subsidiary. Actually they form a unity in which neither is conceivable without the others.

The presentation to follow will be in six main sections, three presenting the primary models of conation, cognition, and affection, and three presenting the secondary models. The psychoanalytic model proper, however, embraces all six in a unity. It is:

THE PSYCHOANALYTIC MODEL

$$\text{Need} \rightarrow \begin{Bmatrix} \text{Need-Satisfying Object} \\ \text{and/or Delay} \end{Bmatrix} \rightarrow \begin{Bmatrix} \text{Need Gratification and/or} \\ \text{Affect Discharge and/or} \\ \text{Ideation (of Goals and Means)} \end{Bmatrix}$$

THE PRIMITIVE MODEL OF CONATION

I submit that the primary psychoanalytic model of conation derives from the following behavior sequence observed in the infant:

restlessness ⟶ *appearance of breast and sucking* ⟶ *subsidence of restlessness* (10, pp. 508-509; 11, IV, pp. 13-21).

Restlessness is conceptualized as tension, and this in turn is conceived as having its source in a drive; breast and sucking are conceptualized as tension-lowering means and activity and are related to the drive as its object and discharge; subsidence of restlessness is conceptualized as tension-subsidence and is related to the drive as its gratification.

Another specifically psychoanalytic conceptualization of this basic observational model is the generalization of tension as *pain* and of tension-subsidence as *pleasure;* the direction implicit to the model is conceptualized as the pain-pleasure principle, or simply as the pleasure principle. Here pleasure and pain are concepts and need not coincide with subjective experience (8, pp. 1-7). In this entire conceptual structure, the drive is that which is usually conceptualized in psychological literature as *motivation*. The pleasure principle is then the conceptual expression of the directional aspect of this motivation.

Yet another conceptualization of the observational model—though not specifically psychoanalytic—generalizes tension as *disequilibrium;* breast and sucking as means and activity directed at *restoring equilibrium;* subsidence of tension as *equilibrium restored*.

The historical connections of the specifically psychoanalytic conceptualizations to Fechner and Helmholz, and of the equilibrium conception to Cannon's homeostasis, cannot be traced here.

From the point of view of psychoanalysis this model is that of discharge activity; from the general psychological point of view, this is the *conative model*. Our next step is to demonstrate that the conceptual model of psychoanalysis derives cognition and affection from the same observational model.

Before turning to the cognitive and affective models, I should like to consider the nature and status of such an observational model. To serve as an effective one it is not necessary that the observational sequence be of general validity, that is, always be present in its entirety whenever any part of it is observed. Indeed, it is not necessary that such a model be based on an *observational* sequence; it can well be based on a hypothetical construction, so long as it systematically co-ordinates the constructs to be used and holds out the hope that a realm of phenomena can rather completely be referred to it.

At this point the question arises: What does "refer to it" mean? It means that verifiable deductions from the model and from the concepts must be possible: this is the portent of the hypothetico-deductive method. Is it necessary that these deductions be expressible in quantitative terms and verifiable experimentally? It would seem that this is desirable, but often neither possible nor necessary. Delbrueck (6) wrote of the evolutionary theory: "[It is] not one proved by decisive experiments, but one that has become more and more inescapable through centuries of accumulated evidence," and he added that at the time of Darwin the theory could not even be put forth in any precise terms. Thus, for the time being, the breadth of relevant observations embraced by the model and the experiential evidence which directly supports it must determine the choice of model. There is sufficient experience to show that the more rigorous, quantitative, and experimentally predictive a model is, the narrower is the range of psychological phenomena for which it has any relevance.

The model so far discussed may be represented as follows:

A DISCHARGE-ACTION (CONATIVE) MODEL

Observational Sequence	Restlessness → Breast and Sucking → Subsidence of Restlessness
1° Abstraction	Tension ⟶ { Tension-Lowering Means and Activity } ⟶ Subsidence of Tension
2° Abstraction (Psychoanalytic)	Pain ⟶ { Pleasure-Gaining Means and Activity } ⟶ Pleasure
3° Abstraction (Psychoanalytic)	Drive ⟶ { Drive Object and Drive Discharge } ⟶ Gratfication
4° Abstraction	Disequilibrium → { Equilibrium-Restoring Means and Activity } ⟶ Equilibrium Restored
5° Partial Abstraction (The Direction of the Model)	⟶ Pleasure-Principle (Directional Aspect of Motivation) ⟶

A further conceptualization, usually termed in the psychoanalytic literature as the economic one, may be added: the tension is conceptualized quasi-quantitatively as the drive-cathexis (charge); the tension-lowering object as the cathected object, the tension-lowering activity as the activity discharging the cathexis; the tension subsidence as the state after the cathexis has been discharged.

A PRIMITIVE MODEL OF COGNITION

Let us now take the observational model and assume that the drive cathexis has mounted to a point where discharge would take place if the drive object were present. Now let the drive object be absent and discharge thus be *delayed*. Let us then assume that under such conditions a hallucinatory image of the memory of the gratification arises. The following model is then arrived at:

Drive ⟶ { Absence of Drive Object: Delay of Discharge } ⟶ { Hallucinatory Image of the Memory of Gratification }

Since this is a model, it could well stand as hypothesized above: its fate depends on its usefulness. However, the concepts within this model will not necessarily be identical with those in the discharge-activity model, unless it is demonstrable that, when drive discharge is delayed, under certain conditions the hallucination phenomena do actually arise. In psychoanalytic literature the model has been derived from the study of precisely such phenomena, particularly dreams. Observations reported by persons who have been on the brink of death by starvation or dehydration, as well as observations on toxic hallucinoses (Meynert's amentia), schizophrenic hallucinations, illusions of normals, daydreams, and so on, further demonstrate that such hallucination phenomena do occur.

Thus, all that is assumed here is that the sequence *restlessness→ absence of breast→hallucinatory image* occurs *in infancy*. It is irrelevant for the model whether or not it does occur; the indirect evidence which makes such an assumption plausible will not be discussed here. But since comparative psychological evidence indicates that infantile perception is diffuse and syncretic (13), the infantile memory of gratification must be conceived as an experience which contains in an undifferentiated form the spatial and temporal context of the drive-object, of the discharge action, and of gratification. Actually study of adult dreams, illusions, and hallucinations demonstrates that in them also the gratification situation is represented by means which can be justifiably labeled syncretic: these means are conceptualized as the Freudian mechanisms of condensation, displacement, substitution, symbolization, etc. [(10) pp. 320-396].

The model is further generalized by assuming that hallucination arises when the memory trace attains full drive cathexis. The drive cathexis is also conceptualized as mobile cathexis: it obeys the pleasure principle in striving for direct discharge; when discharge is not feasible it cathects the memory trace of past discharge (gratification) situation(s); if this is not directly feasible, then, by condensation of various partial memories of gratification, or by displacement to one of them, sufficient cathexis is concentrated to raise to hallucinatory vividness the memory trace of the condensation product, or of that memory trace to which displacement occurred. The entirety of the processes which strive for direct discharge, using mobile cathexes and the mechanisms described, is conceptualized as the *primary process*. The model: drive cathexis → delay of discharge → hallucinatory gratification is in psychoanalytic terms the model of ideation; in general psychological terms it is the model of primary cognition. The direction implicit to it is analogous to the pleasure principle in the model of discharge activity. In the present model it is usually conceptualized as wish fulfilment.

These considerations may be condensed as follows:

A MODEL OF PRIMITIVE COGNITION

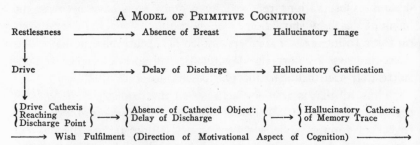

This hallucinatory form of cognition differs from the usual forms of conscious thought in that it does not permit reflection and, in contrast to thought, is as imperious as the drive action: we encounter it in obsessions, hallucinations, monoideic and polyideic fugues and dreams (34). This type of cognition is conceptualized in psychoanalytic literature as ideation, the single contents as ideas or drive representations. The thought organization of this primitive cognition is termed primary-process thinking: it abides by wish fulfilment and the syncretic mechanisms (condensation, displacement, substitution, symbolization), uses sensory (particularly visual) memories, and thus is usually bereft of conjunctions and causal, temporal, and other relationships.

This primitive form of cognition and its conformity with the model proposed above has been abundantly documented in Piaget's work (24, 25), and in the material concerning the comparative psychology of development which H. Werner (41) has integrated. It goes without saying that I have discussed this form of cognition here mainly in its conative relations, and have not attempted to enter the realm of its subtle complexities.

A PRIMITIVE MODEL OF AFFECTS

Let us return once more to the situation in which drive cathexis has mounted to the point where it would discharge, were the drive object present. Assume the drive object to be absent. This is always in fact the first phase of the discharge-activity model, when, before the object appears and activity can take place on it, restlessness prevails. It is this restlessness on which we shall focus our attention now. When the need-satisfying object is absent—or not yet present—the mounting tension may be indicated both by restlessness and by a hallucinatory image of the gratification. We have already seen that the hallucination is conceptualized as drive representation. Should the restlessness also be so conceptualized? It is, in psychoanalytic theory (10, p. 521; 11, pp. 84-136). The drive representation has two aspects: (1) the qualitative one, the idea, which is ultimately the cathected memory trace; (2) the quantitative one, termed the "charge of affect," which comes to expression in those motor and secretory discharge processes which become observable in affect expression. Both the cathexis of the memory trace and the cathexis conceptualized as "charge of affect" are only fragments of the drive cathexis which has accumulated to the point of discharge. The usual relation between the magnitudes of these three divisions of cathexis, inferred from a variety of observations, appears to be as follows:

Drive Cathexis > Affect-Charge Cathexis > Hallucinatory Cathexis of Memory Trace

It should be remembered, however, that we are still within the framework of the primary model, and all the cathexes are, in their quality and origin, drive cathexes.

The distinction between the two kinds of drive representations is necessitated not only by the need to account for the "restlessness" in the observational model, but also by other empirical observations. For instance, in hysteria the ideational representation of the drive may be in abeyance (repressed); affect expression—in the form of hysterical affect-storm or symptom—will take its place; in obsessional neurosis, on the other hand, the ideational representation may remain conscious (obsessional idea), but the affect will usually be in abeyance (repressed or displaced). Hallucinatory idea and restlessness, memory-trace cathexis and affect discharge, are both indicators of and safety valves for mounting drive tension. But they *do not* discharge, as a rule, more than a small fragment of the drive cathexis (5). It is noteworthy that the segregated cathexis conceptualized as "affect charge" strives for immediate discharge as much as does the drive cathexis itself: it is subject to the pleasure principle (10, pp. 535-536).

A PRIMARY MODEL OF AFFECT

Drive
- Drive Cathexis
- Affect Charge → { Affect Discharge (Behavior) Observed or Physiologically Measured } → Affect (Subjectively Felt)
- Cathexis of Memory Trace (Idea)

I shall not dwell on the relation of this model to the James-Lange or Cannon theory and will refer merely to my discussion of the issue elsewhere (30). The segregation of affect charge from the drive cathexis proper, and its discharge as affect *expression* assume that drive discharge is not immediately feasible. This seems to imply a drive-inhibition (conflict) theory of affect. Indeed, to some extent it does. But I shall not dwell on this either, except to point out that such a conception· goes back to Spinoza and even earlier, and to refer to MacCurdy's (23) and my own treatment of this issue (30).

I wish to add that drive discharge may also not be feasible, or only incompletely feasible simply because of the structure of the somatic and psychic organization, and not only because of absence of object or presence of conflict. Here we reach the point where a relation between the segregation of the affect charge and the organic discharge thresholds seems to be suggested. Affect charge would then be defined as that amount of the drive cathexis which can be discharged through the motor and secretory channels of affect expression. Evidence seems to indicate that this amount attains a relative segregation from the rest of the drive cathexis in the course of normal development. Thus, in the discharge thresholds and in this segregation, we encounter—even in the primitive tension-discharge models—structures which maintain rather than discharge tension, and processes due to such tension maintenance. This again cannot be discussed further here.

Thus conation, cognition, and affection—at least in their primitive forms—are derived here from the same observational model. Without entering on the controversy concerning affect and motivation recently opened by Leeper (21), I mention it to bring into relief how unclear even the most conscientious of current psychological thinking is as to the relation of motivation and affect.

CONCERNING PRIMARY AND SECONDARY MODELS

The primary models of action, thought, and affect dealt with the dynamics and economics of cathexes; that is, in their main features they were tension-discharge models. I could have said that these models were stated in terms of energy distributions. The intent to keep the models purely psychological—and the wish not to be faced here with the question, "Do you mean $\frac{1}{2}$ mv^2 when you say energy?"—accounts for the term cathexis. Yet I cannot forego saying that these cathexes do seem to behave in the way energy distributions do (29).

Besides being tension-discharge models, these primitive models did imply certain structural givens: the constitutionally given co-ordination of drive and drive object, the existence of some sort of memory traces, discharge thresholds, and channels of motility and of secretion. Yet they dealt pre-eminently with cathectic dynamics. Now it is obvious that human behavior is not produced from moment to moment in a Battle of Titans of drive cathexes, any more than the human body is produced from moment to moment by metabolic and other processes; only when studied together do function and structure, in their well-known interpenetration, yield the approximate picture we have of the organism. The structures of the psychic apparatus were considered in these primary models, but by implication. Fritz Heider has pointed out (in a personal communication) that one of the salient shortcomings of Lewin's dynamic psychology was that it centered on tensions (dynamics) to the virtual exclusion of structure—on the processes of tension discharge only, to the neglect of those of tension maintenance. Allport (3, pp. 158-169) has rightly insisted that the demonstration of the genetic (onto- or phylogenetic) continuity of motivations accounts neither for the complexity and uniqueness of the adult's motivational structure, nor for the functional autonomy of his motives. Allport seems to consider that a consistent theory, embracing both those phenomena which demand the postulation of the primary model and those which demand models implying functional autonomy, is not feasible. This is precisely what psychoanalytic ego psychology is, and I shall endeavor to present it here (32, 33). Our next task is to center on structure formation, and to present those forms of the psychoanalytic model which include structure. It is inevitable that these models—dealing with far more complex relationships—will be even more schematic than the primitive models.

I should like to interpolate that, for reasons that lie beyond the scope of this paper, I will not deal here with the relevance or irrelevance of this model for phenomena which are variously referred to as those of conscience, ego ideal, etc.

A SECONDARY MODEL OF CONATION

Let us return to the situation in which drive tension has risen to a point close to discharge threshold, with the drive object absent. This hypothetical situation implies the existence of threshold structures, and serves also as a reference point of further structure formation.

The empirical study of motivations shows that besides (a) the motivations which strive for direct discharge and do not tolerate delay, and are conceptualized as drives, there are (b) motivations which are repressed, that is, cut off from direct discharge, as well as (c) motivations which are neither repressed nor undelayably discharge-bent, but amenable in various degrees to postponement of discharge. On the one hand, the drives which have succumbed to the process of repression, or to other defensive operations, may or may not manifest themselves indirectly as altered forms of motivation. On the other hand, the drives which have become amenable to postponement of discharge appear as new forms of motivation. Both sorts of motivations—those deriving from repression of, and those deriving from control of drives—are usually referred to as derivative motivations and are rarely distinguished carefully. The nature of the process of repression and other defenses, and the nature of motivations arising from them are relatively well understood; but the process by which the other type of derivative motivations arises has been little explored.

Let us now concern ourselves with repression. We have seen that the drive abides by the pleasure principle; it strives for direct and complete discharge, to re-establish equilibrium. If the drive object proves "unreliable"—that is, if it is not available regularly within a limited time of delay—then re-establishment of equilibrium by discharge is not possible, and a new method for re-establishing it develops: the organism acts as though the disequilibrium does not exist. In this it follows, on the one hand, the pattern set by the pre-existing discharge threshold; on the other, it actually raises these discharge thresholds by erecting new barriers against discharge. This is achieved by the process of repression (I shall forego treating here of the other defenses) which is conceptualized as follows: against the accumulated drive cathexes, other cathexes —countercathexes—are pitted, establishing an equilibrium on, so to say, a higher level of "potential." Once such a countercathexis (repression) has come about, no discharge occurs, even when the drive object is present. Indeed, the ideational representation, and even the perception of the object is usually barred from consciousness by repression. A variety of observations suggests that the countercathexis derives from the very drive cathexis whose discharge it prevents.

The countercathectic distribution so established appears to behave as though it has a *relative* functional autonomy. The concept "functional autonomy" is used here in Allport's (2) sense. The term *relative* indicates a modification of this concept: the degree to which the countercathectic distribution increases or decreases with —that is, remains dependent upon—the changing intensities of the repressed drive varies from person to person, in time and with situations, and ranges from apparently total independence to that total dependence which becomes manifest in neurotic and psychotic breakdowns (32). The particular importance of this point lies in the fact that countercathectic distributions, just like cathectic distributions, manifest themselves as motivations of behavior: often, in the case of repression, simply as avoidance motivations; in the case of reaction formation, as motivations diametrically opposite to the original drive motivation, etc. Allport is certainly right that such reaction formations are autonomous motivations once they are established, and may even definitively resist change by psychoanalysis (3, p. 165) ; but clinical observation amply shows that the opposite is just as often the case, that psychoanalysis can do away with a motivation of reaction formation character by uncovering its genetic origins and making this form of defense superfluous.

It must be added that these motivations may be just as imperious as the drives themselves, or may be more amenable to delay and detour in reaching their ends. It seems that the degree of relative autonomy is indicated by the degree of such imperiousness. It should be noted also that in the course of normal development these motivations become themselves subject to defensive and delaying controls, just as did the drives. The hierarchic layering of defenses is an empirical datum. It is partly by the hierarchic repetition of this process of defense-structure formation that drives are "tamed" into adult motives; and it is mostly the failure at one point or another of this taming process that gives rise to neurotic, psychotic, or character disturbances.

Turning now to the second kind of derivative motivations, we find that they differ in several salient points from repressed drives: (a) delay does not result in the organism's treating them as non-existent; (b) fortuitous delay is replaced in them by a capability of being delayed in discharge, of being controlled; (c) unlike the repressed drives they are not changed into their opposite, or turned back on the subject, etc., but are discharged when the drive object again becomes available. The process by which these derivative motivations come about is not well understood. It may be conceptualized either as a consequence of repression or as an independent process. In the former case, it would be assumed that the countercathexes which work in repression affect the others also, though not in repressing them but in controlling their discharge. In the latter case, it would be assumed that the discharge threshold becomes modifiable by an arrangement which deploys and withdraws countercathexes in accordance with the availability or unavailability of the drive object. Clinical observation suggests that there is no sharp dichotomy between these two kinds of derivative motivations, but rather that they shade imperceptibly into each other. It also strongly suggests that both the controlling and defensive processes are re-applied to the emerging "tamed" motivations, building a hierarchic series and perpetuating the process of taming; this results in motivations which are increasingly amenable to delay and detour en route to their goal, and in the rise of vicarious subgoals; thus their goal is altered from need satisfaction (tension reduction) to tension maintenance, reality appraisal, and socialization.

This process of "taming" will be more clearly viewed if we keep in mind that these derivative motivations arise from cathectic distributions which alter the drive's discharge thresholds. In effect, these alterations of discharge thresholds are intrapsychic representations of facts of external reality: that is, they modify the drive discharge in the direction of tension maintenance, to discharge only in conformity with reality (33, pp. 723-726).

Though evidence suggests a hierarchic layering of these "taming" processes, it also suggests strongly an interpenetration of the various layers, resulting in an immense complexity of interrelationships. From the point of view of psychoanalysis, this is the genetic history of the rise of ego motivations from drive motivations; mobile drive cathexes abiding by the pleasure principle—that is, discharge bent—are in part transformed into "bound" cathexes (partly employed in the discharge-controlling structures, and partly limited by them in discharge) amenable to delay of discharge and available to the ego for deployment, for which the pleasure principle no longer fully holds, but yields in part to the reality principle. From the point of view of general psychology, this is the genetic history of the relationships between basic needs on the one hand, and strivings, interests, attitudes, opinions, preferences, sets on the other—that is, between the varieties of observed motivations (1, 12). It might be worth noting that Lewin's theory of the dependence of quasi-needs on genuine needs implies such a hierarchic conception, and his theory of the dynamic independence of quasi-needs implies the conception of relative functional autonomy (22 and 33, chap. 5).

The structures here discussed provide for the possibility of delay of discharge, and for both the possibility and means (reality-adapted motivations) of finding in reality the object which permits discharge. The totality of such structures is conceptualized as the ego, while the congeries of immediately discharge-directed drives is conceptualized as the id. The processes amenable to delay and abiding by the reality principle are conceptualized in psychoanalysis as the secondary process; those abiding by the pleasure principle, as the primary process. The above characterization of motivations shows that the ego and id are limiting concepts, and that the processes and structures corresponding to them interpenetrate. It is notable that the secondary process does not dispense with the pleasure principle, but rather modifies it, postpones it, and partially executes it.

Thus, all motivated actions share the tension-reducing character of drive actions. Simultaneously, however, they are also consequences of those tension-maintaining structures and processes which prevent *direct* drive action, and give rise to the derivative motivations of action. Indeed, it seems that in a sense all motivated actions—except drive actions—serve in part to sustain these tension-maintaining structures, to prevent their being swept away by mounting drive tensions. In psychoses, both functional and organic, and in extreme reality situations, these structures fail in a greater or lesser degree (32).

In drives, delay of discharge—except when effected by constitutional discharge thresholds—is fortuitous, in that the environment enforces it; in derivative motivations, delay is guaranteed by internalized—psychological—structures.

The concept of detour has not been defined here. Yet from the studies of Lewin (33, chap. 5) and Tolman (38) as well as from clinical observation (7), one aspect of detour can be readily adduced. Objects other than the need-satisfying or valent object—encountered or sought out in the period of delay— attain secondary valence if action on them will lead to the valent object's becoming available in reality. In other words, means to reach the end object attain part valences of the end object. This state of affairs represents one of the differences between the "mobile cathexes" of the primary process and the "bound cathexes" of the secondary process. While the "mobile" drive cathexes can be displaced only from one to another drive representation, the "bound" or neutralized cathexes can be displaced to anything that serves as a *means* toward the attainment of the object in reality.

The claim that all actions are motivated—that is, cathected by need, and directed toward need-satisfying objects and discharge of need cathexis—may be questioned on the ground that means-actions, habits, and so on, do not conform with this pattern. Lewin's (33, pp. 129-130, 141-143) conception of *ossification,* and Hartmann's (33, pp. 375, 392-396) similar conception of *automotization,* cope with this objection. They show that means actions and habits are not built in the elementalistic fashion of conditioned responses, but are automatized, skeletal, and structuralized forms of originally need-gratifying (motivated) actions (35, 36).

These structuralized means, with which human motivation and action are so invariably intertwined and implemented, are also part and parcel of that cohesive organization of psychological processes and structures which—as was indicated above—is conceptualized as the ego. Let us remind ourselves that such structures as the memory, the perceptual and the motor apparatuses, and the various perceptual and discharge thresholds of the organism, are also integrated within this cohesive organization. It is assumed also that these apparatuses exist before the differentiation of the ego from the id, and serve as nuclei of this process (**14, 32**). It is feasible that psychologies founded on phenomena of associative memory, perception, motility, may be integrated into a psychology built on the model described, but this cannot be pursued here.

In order to arrive at the secondary model of action, a model of psychic structure must be sketched:

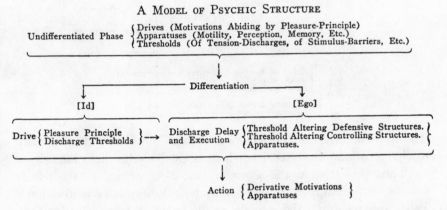

A MODEL OF PSYCHIC STRUCTURE

Implicit in this model is a model of hierarchy of motivations and controls:

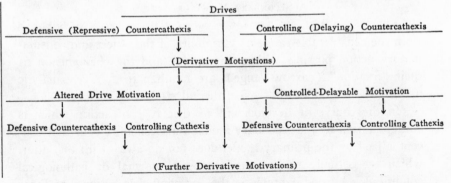

It will also be useful to represent in the form of a schema the conception of relative functional autonomy, and for this purpose the motivational hierarchy is presented in an arbitrarily simplified linear form:

A Model of Relative Functional Autonomy

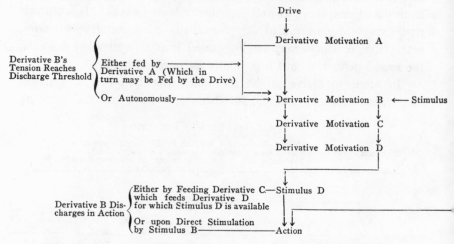

The stimulus here does not create a "drive," but merely triggers the discharge of the drive tension which is close to threshold intensity.

Thus we arrive at the secondary model of action in which the motive, here designated as need, may be any derivative motivation. What appears in the above model as discharge by triggering further derivative motivations, or delay of discharge until Stimulus B has been found, appears in this model as structuralized delay and detour.

A Secondary Model of Action

Need→Structuralized Delay and Detour→Action on Need-Satisfying Object→Need Satisfaction

Both the considerable range of variability of the object and consummatory action possible within this model, and the phenomenon of their "fixation" (narrow range), are familiar from psychoanalytic investigations and Lewin's experimental studies (33, chap. 5).

In the course of development of that type of action which is conceptualized by the secondary model, its ascendance over that conceptualized by the primary model does not do away with the latter, which we actually observe under special normal or pathological conditions. A good example is the somnambule's actions, or those of a person in a monoideic fugue (34).

A Secondary Model of Cognition

It is readily seen that the primary model of cognition *drive cathexis → delay of discharge → drive cathexis of the memory trace* implies a specific set of conditions under which an idea becomes conscious. It should be pointed out that it implies also forms of memory organization, concept formation, and anticipation (28).

In the primary model, consciousness depends upon the drive cathexis of the idea (29, 33). Memory traces are raised to consciousness only in so far as they are drive representations, that is, are associatively related to the situation of gratification; but any memory that is so related can substitute for any other one. Analysis of free associations, slips of the tongue, and dreams shows that memories in the primary process are organized around drives, as their representations. This is conceptualized as the drive organization of memories. Concepts—that is, the belongingness of objects— in the primary process are therefore drive-centered, and thus of the character described by Werner (41) as "things of action" and "physiognomic percepts," or "affective concepts." We may add that the "logic" of the primary process is of the sort Levy-Bruehl described as "participation," Domarus as "paralogic," etc. Anticipations in the primary process appear to reflect the specific relation of the drive and its object: the drive can be said to anticipate its object, since without it no discharge is attained.

In the secondary process, consciousness does not depend merely upon drive cathexis. Even ideas which have drive cathexis without countercathexis may fail to become conscious when other contents command attention: in such cases, the status of the idea is conceptualized as preconscious. Consciousness of both intrapsychic and external stimuli is dependent upon the allotment of *attention-ca-thexis* (hypercathexis). Here consciousness is not a descriptive term but a concept; it is conceived of as a supraordinate sense organ —as such, an apparatus of the ego—which has a determinate amount of bound (neutralized) cathexes at its disposal. Unlike the drive cathexis, this attention cathexis can be commanded by any external as well as intrapsychic stimulus. Thus, to attain consciousness here does not depend upon drive cathexis alone and may not depend on it at all; further, in full consciousness the relationships of the thought which is conscious are also conscious, or at any rate amenable to consciousness (preconscious) (34, 29, 33, pp. 698-699). This is not the case with ideas brought to consciousness by drive cathexes.

The drive organization of memories has also yielded to a different organization. We know from Bartlett's studies (4) that organization in terms of higher level derivative motivations (interests, attitudes, etc.), is characteristic for the secondary process; we also know from studies in problem solving that abstract conceptual organization is also one of its characteristics. We formulate: the drive organization of memories of the primary model yields in the secondary model to a memory organization in terms of frames of reference. Here equivalence of ideas is not defined by what can equally serve as drive representation, but rather by what can equally enhance the chances to discover the object in reality—or so change reality that the object becomes available (10, pp. 533-536, 11, pp. 120-127, 33, pp. 710-712).

In the primary process, concept formation of the physiognomic and "thing of action" types indicated the belongingness of objects only in terms of drive representation or potentiality in promising "pleasure" or "pain"; in the secondary process, this yields to abstract concepts expressing the most general commonalities of the objects of reality (35, 36, pp. 497-580, esp. 641 ff.).

The primitive forms of logic based on physiognomic concepts—such as paralogic, participation, animism (magic), *post hoc ergo propter hoc, pars pro toto*—are replaced by a logic founded on abstract concepts, which is organized in terms of the categories space, time, and causality, and which employs deductive, inductive, and dialectic forms of reasoning (41).

The primitive form of anticipation—wherein a drive tension anticipates the drive object as its sole condition of discharge—develops into complex forms of anticipation which express the range of objects and ideas compatible with sets of simultaneously existing motivations, defenses, reality possibilities, and limitations. The most highly developed forms of these are anticipations codified in the language—that is, in communicated thought—in the form of the conjunctions *(though, however, if,* etc.) which arouse in us general syntactic and specific content anticipation (31, 40, 33, pp. 712-714).

The juxtaposition of these extreme forms of consciousness, memory organization, concept formation, logic, and anticipation, indicates only descriptively the change in the role and nature of thought for which the secondary model of cognition must account.

The change itself is characterized in the psychoanalytic literature (29) as follows:

(1) ideation (hallucinatory drive representation) is an indicator and safety discharge valve of drive tension; it changes into thought, which is experimental action with small cathectic quantities;

(2) ideation uses representations of a drive; it changes into thought, which has available to it—ideally—all memory traces and their relations, for orientation in reality;

(3) ideation is partial discharge, and as such compelling; it changes into thought, which is amenable to delay, detour, and vicarious function;

(4) ideation uses drive cathexes; it changes into thought, which uses neutralized cathexes.

These extremes, however, are connected by a quasi-continuous series of transitory forms (33). The development of these transitory forms of cognition is most directly familiar to us from Piaget's (24, 25) various investigations and from Werner's (41) systematizing work. In psychoanalysis, both clinical material and the studies of Susan Isaacs (17) demonstrate it. This development appears to parallel closely the development of the hierarchy of motivations and defenses discussed above and is particularly dependent upon (a) delay possibility, without which no motive-representing thought arises; (b) neutralization of cathexes, without which the motive-representing thought cannot be raised to consciousness except when the motive tension has reached threshold intensity.

Here too, just as we have seen in regard to action, a relative functional autonomy obtains: a thought may be aroused as a response by a stimulus's setting off any appropriate derivative motivation, without relation to any motivation more basic. And just as in action, the thought may directly arouse other thoughts and seek the object of the motivation by using neutralized cathexes, or it may set off further derivative motivations, and indirectly through them other thoughts, and so seek the object.

There is here an additional point which cannot be by-passed. The memory connections, the conceptual belongingness, and the anticipations which have once arisen in the interplay of motivations and in the quest for the object which satisfies simultaneously several effective motives (overdetermɨɴation) are not lost with the progress of psychological development; rather, by again and again recurring in approximately similar situations, they become structuralized (Hartmann: "automatized"; Lewin: "ossified") and available as fixed tools, quasi-stationary apparatuses, for use in the thought process. The more or less idiosyncratic sets and instrumental attitudes (Allport, 1), as well as the conjunctions of the language—of so high an order of social agreement—are such ossified anticipations. The "popular responses" on association and other projective tests are such automatized memorial and conceptual connections (27, 28). The thought forms of general syntax and logic also develop thus. In contrast to the conditioning conception, we have here a conception in which the simple automatic connections are simplified automatizations of complex interactions of motivations. The derivative motivations—as we have seen—come about as modifications of more basic motivations by the internalization of environmental limitations. The development of the fixed structures of thought amounts similarly to internalization of environmental conditions and thus guarantees the reality adaptedness and socialized character of thought. The role of communication in this process is salient but cannot be discussed here. Piaget's studies and the clinical studies of identification provide the initial material for conceptualizing the role of communication (interpersonal relationship) in the development of reality adaptation and socialization. The processes referred to here are usually treated under the heading of "learning." But the conventional theories of learning usually disregard both the motivational and the structure-creating aspects of these processes (33, pp. 723-728).

In the ascendance of the secondary process over the primary, the latter, together with the transitory forms between the two, survives and manifests itself—though modified—in wishful thinking, daydreams, dreams, etc., under normal conditions; in illusions, preoccupations, hypnotic phenomena, etc., under extreme conditions; and in delusions, hallucinations, obsessions, pseudo-memories, etc., under pathological conditions.

We may now sketch the "secondary model of cognition":

A SECONDARY MODEL OF COGNITION

{ Need (Any Derivative Motivation)

↓

{ Delay of Discharge Guaranteed
{ by Intrapsychic Regulations

↓

{ Setting Off of Further Derivative Needs [E.g., Quasi-Needs (Lewin)]
{ or Directly Initiating a Thought Process (Using Neutralized Cathexes
{ and Taking Detours through Conceptually and Memorially Related
{ Thoughts) Regulated by Means of Automatized Anticipations, Concepts,
{ and Memorial Connections Relevant to the Need.

↓

{ Thought Process Development, Using Ever-Narrowing Anticipations and
{ Conceptually Related Ideas as Means to the End of Reaching, in Reality,
{ the Need-Satisfying Object or the Pathways Leading to It.

↓

{ Consciousness of the Object and of the Ways to Reach It in Reality.

A SECONDARY MODEL OF AFFECT

Space permits only a perfunctory treatment of the secondary model of affects.

The observational facts for which a secondary model of affects must account are in the main clinical. They comprise the continuum ranging from elemental discharges (e.g., joy and rage) through mild conscious experiences of feeling tone (e.g., pleasantness and unpleasantness) to "cold affects" which hardly differ from the intellectual experience that a given feeling would be appropriate (30). The model must also account for the fact that this continuum is by no means as simple and linear as it may seem. Elemental affect discharges comprise expressive movements, visceral and secretory processes, emotion felt, and consciousness of the relation to a stimulus; but in each of the various forms of affects any of these constituents, or any combinations of them, may be absent. The model should also account for the observational fact that affects can become chronic either in their totality (e.g., in some forms of anxiety), or in their physiological concomitants (e.g., in functional hypertension), or in their feeling tone (e.g., in moods), or in their expressive movements (e.g., in the stereotyped frozen smiles or angrily set jaws, or in individually characteristic postures) (9, 20). Furthermore, it must account for the histrionic affects, the "as if" affects which are subjectively experienced as "not genuine," the affects which are excessively indulged in, as seen in schizoid personalities and disorders. Finally, of the many other varieties of affects to be accounted for, we might mention those involved in the experience of wit or humor (11a, 19a).

First, the secondary model of affects conceptualizes the continuum referred to above as affect forms related to the delay in discharge of derivative motivations. As in drives, so in these derivative motivations there appear affect discharges which serve as safety valves and indicators of their increasing tension. *Secondly,* it conceptualizes the absence of the various components of affects as the result of their having succumbed to repression, isolation, or displacement. *Thirdly,* it conceptualizes the chronicity of affects, or of certain of their components, as the result of the segregation, autonomy, and automatization of their affect charge; this change can be triggered either momentarily by derivative motivations, or continuously by processes other than the threshold intensity of the motivation corresponding to it. This is the case in anxiety, where the ego plays the triggering role (9), and in guilt and depression (20), where it is played by the superego—a structure which here remains undefined. *Finally,* it may be mentioned that, under specific conditions, the affect-charge cathexes may play a motivational role. This, however, is by no means so general that it would make tenable Leeper's and Duffy's attempts at offering a motivational theory of affects. The essential relation of affect to motivation is that the affect charge is a part of the motivational cathexis, i.e., constitutes as much of the motivational cathexis as can find discharge through the motor and secretory channels proper to affect discharge.

Since this treatment is perfunctory and does not meet many of the issues and theories customarily presented in discussions of affects, the model I present here is even more sketchy than the others presented above:

THE MODEL OF AFFECT DEVELOPMENT

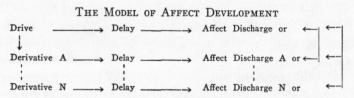

THE SECONDARY MODEL OF AFFECT

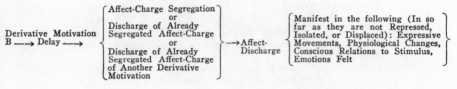

CONCLUSION

The model presented here is characterized by the following features:

(a) it does away with the arbitrary segregation of conation, cognition, and affection;

(b) it has the scope to do away with the arbitrary segregation of memory, association, imagination, etc., conceptualizing them as various aspects of thought organization;

(c) it has the potentiality to integrate within its framework the motor and the perceptual processes—a function which was hardly hinted at in the present sketch;

(d) it takes account of motivation (function) as well as structure;

(e) its crucial concepts—delay and detour—may serve as a bridge between the extremes of animal psychological observations, and cybernetic, goal-seeking, feedback mechanisms;

(f) its pervasively motivational character implies Allport's "intention" and Brentano's "intentionality";

(g) it is genetically oriented, and thus capable of encompassing developmental and comparative psychological phenomena;

(h) it is a purely psychological model, cast to systematize psychological data—observational and introspective—no matter how remote from any neurologically or physiologically tangible phenomena. Yet it does not exclude the hope that, in the distant future, the gap may considerably narrow between these psychologically systematized observations and those neurologically and physiologically systematized.

REFERENCES

1. ALLPORT, G. Attitudes. In Carl Murchison (ed.), *A handbook of social psychology.* Worcester: Clark Univ. Press, 1935. Pp. 798-844.

2. ALLPORT, G. *Personality.* New York: Holt, 1937.

3. ALLPORT, G. *The nature of personality: selected papers.* Cambridge: Addison-Wesley Press, 1950.

4. BARTLETT, F. *Remembering: a study in experimental and social psychology.* Cambridge: Cambridge University Press, 1932.

5. BRIERLY, M. Affects in theory and practice. *Int. J. Psycho-Anal.,* 1937, **18**, 256-268.

6. DELBRUECK, M. A physicist looks at biology. *Transactions of the Connecticut Acad. of Arts and Sciences,* 1949, **38**, 173-190.

7. FRENCH, T. Goal, mechanism and integrative field. *Psychosomat. Med.,* 1941, **3**, 226-252.

8. FREUD, S. *Beyond the pleasure principle.* London: Int. Psychoanalytic Press, 1922.

9. FREUD, S. *The problem of anxiety.* New York: Psychoanalytic Quart. Press, 1936.

10. FREUD, S. The interpretation of dreams. In *The basic writings.* New York: Modern Library, 1938.

11. FREUD, S. *Collected papers.* London: Hogarth, 1946.

11ᵃTREAD, S. *Collected papers,* V. London: Hogarth, 1950.

12. GIBSON, J. A critical review of the concept of set in contemporary experimental psychology. *Psychol. Bull.,* 1941, **38**, 781-817.

13. HARTMANN, H. Ich-Psychologie und Anpassungsproblem. *Int. Z. Psa. Imago,* 1939, **24**, 62-135.

14. HARTMANN, H. Comments on the psychoanalytic theory of instinctual drives. *Psychoanal. Quart.,* 1948, **17**, 368-388.

15. HARTMANN, H., KRIS, E., AND LOEWENSTEIN, R. Comments on the formation of psychic structure. *Psychoanal. Study of the Child,* 1946, **2**, 11-38.

16. HEBB, D. O. *Organization of behavior.* New York: John Wiley & Sons, 1949.

17. ISAACS, S. *Intellectual growth in young children.* London: Routledge & Sons, 1945.

18. KRECH, D. Dynamic systems as open neurological systems. *Psychol. Rev.,* 1950, **57**, 345-361.

19ᵃKRIS, E. Ego development and the comic. *Int. J. Psycho-Anal.,* 1938, **19**, 77-90.

19ᵇKRIS, E. On preconcious mental processes. In *Organization and pathology of thought,* pp. 474-493. See particularly pp. 485-491.

20. LANDAUER, K. Affects, passions and temperament. *Int. J. Psycho-Anal.,* 1938, **19**, 388-415.

21. LEEPER, R. A motivational theory of emotion to replace 'emotion as disorganized response.' *Psychol. Rev.,* 1948, **55**, 5-21.

22. LEWIN, K. Kriegslandschaft. *Z. Psychol.,* 1917, **12**, 440-447.

23. MacCURDY, J. *The psychology of emotion, morbid and normal.* New York: Harcourt, Brace, 1925.

24. PIAGET, J. Children's philosophies. In *A handbook of child psychology.* Worcester: Clark University Press, 1931.

25. PIAGET, J. Le probleme biologique de l'intelligence. In *La naissance de l'intelligence.* Neuchatel and Paris: Delachaux and Niestle, 1936. See also Chap. 7 in **33**.

26. RAPAPORT, D. Principles underlying projective techniques. *Charact. & Pers.,* 1942, **10**, 213-219.

27. RAPAPORT, D. Principles underlying non-projective tests of personality. *Ann. N. Y. Acad. Sc.,* 1946, **66**, 643-652.

28. RAPAPORT, D., GILL, M., AND SCHAFER, R. *Diagnostic psychological testing.*

2 vols. Chicago, Year Book Publishers, 1945-1946. See particularly pp. 385-389.

29. RAPAPORT, D. On the psychoanalytic theory of thinking. *Int. J. Psycho-Anal.,* 1950, **31**, 1-10.

30. RAPAPORT, D. *Emotions and memory* (2nd ed.). New York: Int. Univ. Press, 1950.

31. RAPAPORT, D. Paul Schilder's contribution to the theory of thinking. *Int. J. Psycho-Anal.,* 1951, **32**, 291-301.

32. RAPAPORT, D. The autonomy of the ego. *Menninger Bull.,* 1951, **15**, 113-123.

33. RAPAPORT, D. Ego psychology and the problem of adaptation. Chap. 19 in H. Hartmann, *Organization and pathology of thought.* New York: Columbia University Press, 1951.

34. RAPAPORT, D. States of consciousness, a psychopathological and psychodynamic view. In Abramson (ed.), *Problems of consciousness,* II. Macy Foundation Symposium, 1951. (In Press.)

35. SCHILDER, P. *Brain and personality.* New York: Nerv. & Ment. Dis. Pub., 1931. See particularly Chap. VII.

36. SCHILDER, P. In *Organization and pathology of thought.* See **33**, above.

37. SCHROEDINGER, E. *What is life?* New York: Macmillan, 1947.

38. TOLMAN, E. *Purposive behavior in animals and men.* Berkeley: University of California Press, 1932. See particularly Chaps. 11 & 12.

39. TOLMAN, E. The psychology of social learning. *J. soc. Issues,* 1949, **5**, 3-18.

40. VARENDONCK, J. The psychology of daydreams. In *Organization and pathology of thought,* **33**, pp. 451-473. See particularly pp. 461, 466-467.

41. WERNER, H. *Comparative psychology of mental development.* New York: Harper, 1940.

Comments on Theoretical Models

Illustrated by the Development of a Theory of Conflict Behavior*

NEAL E. MILLER

Department of Psychology and Institute of Human Relations, Yale University

THIS PAPER will begin with a few general comments on theory. Then some of the main points in the commentary will be illustrated by an example of the development and testing of a theory of approach-avoidance conflict behavior. Finally, the discussion will include a brief résumé of recent extensions of the theory to displacement, psychotherapy, and psychological effects of certain drugs. References will also be made to new experimental evidence relevant to these extensions.

GENERAL COMMENTS ON THEORY

Criteria of a scientific theory. A system of symbols (in either verbal or other form) can properly be called a model or theory if, and only if, one can use it to make rigorous deductions about some of the consequences of different sets of conditions (9, 19). High-school geometry is a familiar example. It consists of a set of definitions and axioms, or in other words, terms and rules for manipulating the terms. This relatively limited number of basic terms and rules can be used to deduce the consequences of a great number of different conditions. Such a deduction is illustrated in the proof of the Pythagorean theorem. From the condition "given a right triangle" one can deduce that "the square on the hypotenuse is equal to the sum of the squares of the other two sides." Everyone who has mastered the system will agree on this deduction.

The first test of a model or theory is its ability to mediate rigorous deductions analogous to the proof of the Pythagorean theorem or the solution of an algebraic equation. It is obvious that many cur-

*The author thanks Mr. E. J. Murray and Mr. W. H. Kessen for reading the manuscript and making helpful suggestions.

rent "theories" or "models" in psychology fail to meet this criterion. They should be classified as points of view, articles of faith or intuitions—but *not* as theoretical models. Such pseudo-theories or pseudo-models may be useful in motivating or guiding the research of their proponents. They may eventually lead to the development of a true theory, or they may obstruct progress by giving a false sense of problem solution.

A theoretical model can be created as an intellectual game without any reference to specific phenomena in the "real world." In order for a theory to be useful, the scientist must have some relatively unambiguous way of relating the terms in the theory to the phenomena that interest him. For example, in order to use the Pythagorean theorem in estimating how long a fence is needed to cut diagonally across a field, one needs some way of relating the conditions of the farmer's field to those specified in geometry or, in other words, of determining how long the sides of the field are, that they are straight, and that the angle between them is 90 degrees. Finally one needs some way of relating the deduction of the length of the hypotenuse to the length of the fence. As Hull (9) has said, the chain of intervening theoretical constructs must be firmly anchored at both ends.

This linking of the antecedent conditions and consequent deductions of the theory to observable phenomena is accomplished by definitions. Carnap (4) has called such definitions *reduction sentences* because they reduce the terms of the theory to observables. An operational definition is a special kind of reduction sentence. Thus, in the example we have been considering, the theoretical terms of geometry are linked to the practical conditions of the farmer's field by the operations of sighting down straight lines, measuring length, and measuring angles. Often psychological theories fail to be useful because there is no practical way of relating both the antecedent conditions and the deduced consequences of the theory with events that can be identified unambiguously and publicly.

Carnap (4) has pointed out that many of the definitions which scientists use to connect theoretical terms with observables are incomplete. They may be called *partial definitions*. The advantage of the partial definition is that it does not completely limit the meaning of the term once and for all but allows room for expanding the meaning, step by step, on the basis of accumulated knowledge. For example, temperature may be defined by the expansion of a column of mercury. This definition is rigorous in that the appropriate use of a mercury thermometer is sufficient to determine the temperature of a body; it is partial in that many other effects, in addition to the expansion of mercury, may be linked with temperature and either used as measures of it or deduced as consequences of it. Examples of other phenomena linked with temperature are changes in the electrical resistance of a wire, the voltage produced by a thermocouple, and the spectrum of emitted light. As long as any room is left for adding such other effects as may be usefully related to temperature, the definition is not complete but partial.

In short, the use of a scientific theory involves three steps: (a) the unambiguous connection of a series of observable antecedent conditions with the terms of the theory by means of definitions, (b) the rigorous derivation of deductions by manipulating the terms according to specific rules, and (c) linking the terms in the deductions with observable phenomena by means of definitions.[1] When an observable consequence of a certain set of conditions is deduced in advance, it is called a *prediction;* when it is derived after the fact, it is called an *explanation* (8).

Application limited by ability to specify conditions. Some of the greatest difficulties of applying theory to phenomena of practical importance arise at the point of linking the antecedent conditions in the practical situation with those specified in the theoretical model. It may be difficult to measure the conditions in the practical situation; they may vary in unknown ways or be too complex for the theory to handle.

Even the best of our natural-science theories are severely limited in this way. Most of the physicist's exact predictions deal with quite special and precisely defined conditions, such as a freely falling body in a vacuum with precise instruments available to measure distance and time. No physicist will even attempt to predict where

---

[1] It should be noted that the same term may appear in both the antecedent conditions and the consequent deductions. Thus, in the example of the Pythagorean theorem, the hypotenuse and the base are both measured in the same units of length. Furthermore, the length of the hypotenuse may be predicted in one situation but used as an antecedent condition in a different situation.

a given snowflake will fall in a blizzard, although snowflakes are much more common and of much greater practical importance than freely falling bodies in a vacuum. Even if you give the physicist the far simpler problem of trying to increase the percentage of snowflakes falling in a given area, he will not give you an immediate answer. He will want either to make extensive empirical field tests or to construct a wind tunnel and make special studies of the effects of various shapes and arrangements of objects affecting the flow and turbulence of the air. Similarly, in spite of all the theoretical knowledge and empirical experience of the automobile industry, every new model of automobile needs extensive road tests. Often the engineer applying physical science allows himself factors of safety of more than 200% to take care of uncontrolled variations in the conditions. He may also have to supplement theory with those less precisely verbalized but highly significant results of experience which may be described as art or skill.

Finally, there are a great many problems that the physicist will not even attempt to solve. The power of his theory to predict is often severely limited by the complexity or ambiguity of the antecedent conditions. It is unfortunate that social scientists (or even physicists talking about social science) sometimes fail to recognize similar limitations and misuse the prestige of their science to give confident answers to important problems that their theories cannot resolve.

Importance of theory. Does this mean that the physicist's theories are useless? Obviously not! Though many problems of great practical importance cannot be solved, others can. And between these two extremes is a wide range of problems for which theory is enormously useful even though it cannot give any immediate solution. For these problems the theory is useful (a) in greatly restricting the range of trial and error by ruling out impossible alternatives, (b) in suggesting general lines of attack that would not otherwise be thought of and tried, and (c) in devising techniques for analyzing conditions and measuring results. In many areas a physicist will start out far behind the layman who has had practical experience, but, after a period of empirical trial and error guided by theory, will end up with a superior solution.

Inevitability of hypotheses. As a hangover from their rebellion against the speculations of their philosophical ancestors some social scientists are extremely suspicious of any theory. They say that we should dispense with all theory and just get the facts. This sounds like hard common sense. But it fails to take account of the fact that some selection must inevitably be made among the *infinite* number of facts that could be observed.

For example, two prominent social scientists claimed that they were getting the facts without any harmful bias from theory because they were taking motion pictures of events in a primitive culture. But they did not have cameras pointing from all possible angles at all possible events, day and night, for all of the days in the year. Such a procedure would have filled all of the museums in the world with film, each foot of which would have contained enough facts—the distance between each of the fingers, the number of leaves on the tree and stones on the ground—to keep a cataloguer busy for years. The investigators had to choose where to point the camera, when to push the button that started it, and what to measure and count on the film.

With an infinite sea of potential facts, most of them completely irrelevant, all investigators are forced to make a drastic selection. If this selection is not made consciously on the basis of an explicitly formulated theory, it is made unconsciously on the basis of perceptual habits and the folklore of the culture. It is impossible to avoid selecting data on the basis of some sort of a hypothesis.

The theorist also starts with the folklore of the culture. But he tries to make it as explicit as possible. This helps him to test it and improve on it.

Generality and power. The great power of good theoretical constructs comes from their generality. When an attempt is made to formulate a law by specifying one observable phenomenon directly as a function of one or more immediately observable conditions, it is often found that such laws are highly specific. For example, taking the type of substance as the condition and floating or sinking as the phenomenon, we need a whole series of laws such as wood floats, oil floats, paraffin floats, stones sink, metals sink, etc. Furthermore there are likely to be exceptions, e.g., teakwood sinks and pumice stone floats. Thus the scientist is driven toward more abstract formulations, using terms such as *density* which do not refer directly to anything that is immediately observable. Stated in such terms, the law becomes: "A substance will float if its density is less than that of water." This law is more general; the specific cases, including the troublesome exceptions, may be deduced from it and a knowledge of the relevant conditions, namely the weight and volume. Then, as Feigl (7) has pointed out, the more general laws formulated in this more abstract way may in turn be deduced from still more general principles formulated in terms still further removed from the immediate observables until finally we reach something like the Maxwell electromagnetic wave theory or the general theory of relativity.

In this connection it is interesting to note that in psychology there seems to be some correlation between trying to limit oneself to direct functional relationships between immediately observable measures, with a minimum of theoretical formulation, and writing summaries of the following general form: w and x have secured positive results; y and z have secured negative ones; it is too early to draw any general conclusion.

Finally it should be noted that the predictions that can be made on the basis of direct correlations between immediately observable events are limited either to situations that have already been encountered before or to simple extrapolation or interpolation of established relationships. The more abstract forms of theoretical formulation allow one to make predictions for situations that are more novel. It can be seen that this difference is parallel to the fact that logical learning is usually more economical and flexible than rote learning. Emphasizing the value of more abstract theoretical formulations does not mean that we discount the importance of determining the direct relationships between immediately observable phenomena. Science must start at this level, but it does not stop there.

Sometimes an assumption is made to help account for a particular set of observations. Then it is found that additional deductions, which also flow from this assumption, account for other quite different observations. This is a thrilling experience for the theorist. It confirms his belief that there are uniformities in nature which are amenable to parsimonious description.

Rigor vs. range. The physicist is not disturbed by his inability immediately to create an atomic-powered airplane or the biologist by his inability completely to arrest senescence and death. By contrast, some social scientists feel that their theories ought to produce immediate solutions to the most pressing problems of our time. They are overly distraught if their theories cover only a limited range of phenomena. Thus they are motivated to extend the range of their theories at the sacrifice of rigor until their theories become so loose that they are meaningless. Though science strives toward generality, it is not necessary to have one all-embracing theory. Physics made a great deal of progress while it was still divided into separate, more limited theories such as those of mechanics, hydrostatics, heat, electricity, and optics.

While different theories should not be scrambled illogically together in one grand eclectic hash, there is nothing to prevent the scientist from using entirely different models to deal with different aspects of his theoretical and practical problems. In short, rigorous but limited models can be extremely useful.

Rigor vs. immortality. The value of a theory is not measured by the length of its life. A theory can be wrong and still lead to progress. In Smyth's (17) lucid sketch of the history of physics from X-rays to nuclear fission one of the most striking facts is the short life-span of the theories. Almost as soon as each theory was clearly formulated, it led to new observations which proved its inadequacy and demanded the formulation of a new theory which in turn was quickly shown to be wrong. But this was not bad; the period showed rapid and fundamental advances. Such advances were made possible by the fact that the theories were stated so clearly and exactly that it was easy to prove them wrong and correct them.

As Professor Hull has often said: "It takes courage to state a theory clearly and exactly." Anyone who tries to do this will find that he is flying in the face of strong motivation to protect himself by hedging, becoming vague, or remaining conventional. It is an honorable scientific achievement to state a theory so rigorously that it can be quickly disproved.

Predictability of human behavior. We have emphasized the fact that even the best models of physical science are severely limited to relatively simple and specifiable conditions. From this limitation one should not jump to the conclusion that the conditions affecting human personality must inevitably be so complex and indeterminately variable that the use of any rigorous theoretical models will be impossible.

Large portions of human behavior are highly predictable. For example, a driver on the highway may bet his life 100 times within an hour on the predictability of human behavior—that none of 100 drivers coming the opposite way at a closing speed of eighty miles per hour will suddenly decide to swerve in front of his car. In the case of two cars approaching each other on an open highway, the relevant conditions—e.g., previous training, visual cues and the fear of the consequences of a head-on collision—are clear-cut enough so that behavior is highly predictable. In other cases the conditions are less clear-cut—vision obscured by a curve, caution reduced by alcohol, or competing motivation induced by extreme fatigue— and behavior is less predictable.

Similarly, the author has been held up by a considerable number of mechanical failures, hotboxes, broken driving rods, washouts, etc., in the course of extensive experience riding on railroads; he has never been delayed because the engineer decided to get out and pick daisies. The mechanical behavior of the physical structure of the railroad was less predictable than the human behavior of the engineer. Without an enormous amount of highly predictable behavior, human social life would be impossible.

The reliability of empirical predictions in many areas of human behavior suggests that it should be just as susceptible to rigorous theoretical systematization as certain limited types of physical phenomena.

Development and Extension of Conflict Theory

An analysis of approach-avoidance conflict behavior may be taken as a concrete example of the systematic development of a theoretical model relevant to certain problems of personality. Only enough of the chief logical units will be presented to allow the reader to follow the argument; no attempt will be made to present the model in a complete, elegant form. Instead the aim will be to bring out as simply as possible how the theory was developed and extended.

First the basic assumptions and certain partial definitions will be presented. Then it will be shown how the simplest deductions, each involving a single basic assumption and partial definitions, were tested in controlled experimental situations. After this the manner in which slightly more complex deductions were made and verified will be indicated as well as how the model was extended from conflict behavior to displacement, and how extremely simple and then slightly more complex deductions from this extension were verified in controlled experimental situations. Finally, we shall consider extensions to the effects of drugs and to complex clinical phenomena of the type encountered in psychotherapy. More details of certain aspects of this model have been presented elsewhere (6, 11, 12).

Basic assumptions. In its simplest form the model begins with the following five basic assumptions:

(A) The tendency to approach a goal is stronger the nearer the subject is to it. This will be called the *gradient of approach.*

(B) The tendency to avoid a feared stimulus is stronger the nearer the subject is to it. This will be called the *gradient of avoidance.*

(C) The strength of avoidance increases more rapidly with nearness than does that of approach. In other words, the gradient of avoidance is *steeper* than that of approach.

(D) The strength of tendencies to approach or avoid varies with the strength of the drive upon which they are based. In other words, an increase in drive raises the height of the entire gradient.

(E) When two incompatible responses are in conflict, the stronger one will occur.

In order to make use of a simple form of graphic exposition, it is necessary to make an additional assumption, namely, that the gradients may be represented graphically by curves having the characteristics described by the assumptions (e.g., a continuous negative slope which is steeper for avoidance than for approach at each point above the abscissa), and that all deductions which are general to curves meeting these specifications are legitimate. It will be noted that the graphic analysis has the advantage of clarity and immediate intelligibility. It has the disadvantage of forcing one to be more specific than one wants to be: for example, one selects a straight line as the simplest example of the family of possible curves, and then awkwardly disclaims the implied assumption of linearity by pointing out that the deductions would hold for any curves with the specified properties of negative slope.

Partial definitions and experimental verification. Now let us consider some simple experiments performed by Brown (3) to test the model. One group of albino rats was trained to run down a short alley to secure food when hungry; another group was trained in the same alley to avoid the distinctive place at which it received an electric shock. Each animal wore a little harness connected to a recording device in such a way that his strength of pull, when stopped at a specific point in the alley, could be measured in grams.

In order to relate the conditions in this experiment to those in the theoretical model, it is necessary to make the following partial definitions:

(A) That the term *nearness* as used in the assumptions can be measured by spatial distance in the experimental alley.

(B) That the animals running to food are being trained to *approach* under the motivation of hunger.

(C) That the animals running away from shock are being trained to *avoid* under the motivation of fear.

(D) That greater amounts of food deprivation, up to a limit of at least forty-eight hours, produce greater *strengths of hunger drive.*

(E) That greater strengths of electric shock, within the limits used, produce *greater strengths of fear drive.*

In order to relate the deductions to a specific type of behavior it is necessary to make one more partial definition:

(F) That within the limits of the animal's capacity to pull, there is some sort of a monotonic positive relationship between strength of response tendency and strength of pull.

With the aid of these partial definitions it is possible to make specific predictions and to test separately the applicability of each of the first four basic assumptions in the theoretical model to the controlled experimental situation. When Brown (3) did this, he confirmed the deductions by finding: (a) the animals that were stopped nearer the food pulled harder than those stopped farther from it; (b) the animals that were stopped nearer the place where they had been shocked pulled harder than those stopped farther from that place; (c) the strength of pull for avoidance increased more rapidly with nearness than did that of approach; (d) increasing the strength of the shock used in the original training increased the strength of pull at both the near and the far points on the avoidance gradient, and increasing the hours of food deprivation increased the strength of pull on the approach gradient.

The next deductions to be verified were somewhat more complex ones involving the interaction of approach and avoidance. The theoretical analysis is summarized graphically in Figure 1. The

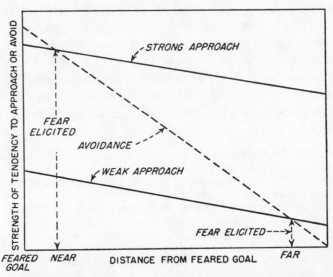

FIG. 1. Graphic representation of an approach-avoidance conflict and of the effect of increasing the strength of the motivation to approach. When the point at which the gradients intersect is between the subject and the goal, approach is stronger than avoidance. Therefore the subject moves toward the goal. When he passes the point of intersection, avoidance becomes stronger than approach; so he stops and turns back. Increasing the strength of the drive motivating approach raises the height of the entire gradient of approach. Since this causes the point of intersection to occur nearer the goal, the subject approaches nearer. Since this nearer point is higher on the gradient of avoidance, more fear is elicited.

These deductions hold only for the range within which the two gradients intersect. It is only for the sake of simplicity that the gradients are represented by straight lines in these diagrams. Similar deductions could be made on the basis of any curves that have a continuous negative slope which is steeper for avoidance than for approach at each point above the abscissa.—Figure adapted from Miller (11).

parts of the diagram referring to "strong approach" and "fear elicited" should be ignored for the time being. It can be seen that at the farthest distance from the goal, the weak approach is stronger than the avoidance. Thus one would expect the animal to start approaching the goal. As the animal gets nearer the goal he eventually reaches a point at which avoidance becomes stronger than approach. At this point he should stop. Thus we deduce that the

subject should go part way and then stop. It is also apparent that
as the strength of approach is increased (see strong approach), the
point at which the gradients cross and the subject should stop is
moved nearer to the goal. Similarly from Figure 2 it can be seen

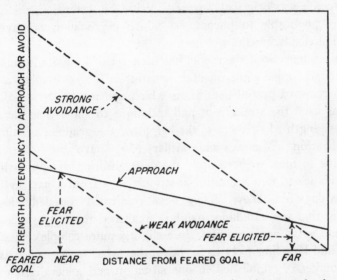

Fɪɢ. 2. Graphic representation of the way decreasing the strength of motivation to avoid affects an approach-avoidance conflict. Reducing the strength of
motivation to avoid lowers the height of the entire gradient of avoidance and
causes the point of intersection to move nearer to the feared goal. Therefore
the subject approaches nearer to the feared goal. When he is nearer, more
fear is elicited.

These deductions hold only for the range within which the two gradients
intersect. It is only for the sake of simplicity that the gradients are represented
by straight lines in these diagrams. Similar deductions could be made on the
basis of any curve that has a continuous negative slope which is steeper for
avoidance than approach at each point above the abscissa.—Figure adapted from
Miller (11).

that decreases in the strength of avoidance should cause the subject
to approach nearer to the goal. Experimental tests in a simple approach-avoidance conflict situation have verified all of these deductions. Approaching part way and then stopping is characteristic of
subjects in such a situation, and increases in the strength of hunger
or decreases in the strength of fear cause the subjects to approach
nearer to the feared goal (11).

Extension to include displacement. Thus far *nearness* has been
defined in terms of spatial distance. One may extend the scope of

the model by making an additional assumption, namely, that gradients of stimulus generalization behave in the same way as gradients of spatial distance. This assumption expands the partial definition of *nearness* to include qualitative similarity to the situation in which the response was originally learned. With this extension, the model becomes applicable to phenomena which psychoanalysts have described as displacement.

This extension of the model has been verified on albino rats in a number of simple experimental situations. These involve a few straightforward partial definitions which will not be listed. Brown (2) has used the strength-of-pull technique to show that increases in the strength of drive raise the height of the gradient of stimulus generalization. Murray and Miller (16) have used the same technique to measure separately the generalization of approach and of avoidance to new stimulus situations, e.g., from a narrow black to a wide white alley. They have confirmed the deduction by showing that the avoidance habit is weakened more by generalization than is the approach one. In a slightly more complex situation, Miller and Kraeling (14) have shown that when an approach-avoidance conflict is established in one situation and generalized to another somewhat similar situation, the subjects are more likely to approach the dangerous goal in the new situation than in the original one. This is exactly what would be deduced from the assumption that the avoidance is weakened more by generalization than the approach. It will be recognized as similar to the clinical phenomenon of displacement in which, for example, a person generalizes aggression more strongly to a scapegoat than he does the responses inhibiting the aggression.

Miller (12) has used this extension of the model to derive eight deductions (with five corollaries) describing specific ways in which the phenomena of displacement should be affected by various conditions. In general, clinical evidence seems to confirm these deductions. Whiting and Sears (20) and their students have applied the model to predictions of children's behavior in projective doll-play situations and secured experimental verification of a number of deductions.

Effects of alcohol and barbiturates. Conger (5) has extended the model in a different direction by adding the assumption that alcohol produces a greater reduction in fear motivating avoidance than in hunger (and presumably other primary drives) motivating approach. He has confirmed the simplest deductions from this extension by measuring approach and avoidance separately in a controlled experimental situation. He has shown that alcohol produces a greater reduction in the strength of pull of frightened rats avoiding the place where they had previously received electric shock than of hungry rats approaching food. He also tested the more complex situation in which approach and avoidance are operating simultaneously. He trained hungry rats to approach food, and then threw them into an approach-avoidance conflict by giving them electric shocks at the goal. He verified the deduction by finding that they were more likely to go back to the food after receiving injections of alcohol than of normal saline. Both Conger (5) and Dollard and Miller (6) have also used this extension of the model to explain some of the perplexing social effects of alcohol.

Bailey and Miller (1) and Dollard and Miller (6) have extended the model along similar lines by assuming that barbiturates, such as sodium amytal, produce a greater reduction in the strength of the fear motivating avoidance than in other drives motivating approach. A deduction from this assumption has been used to explain an observation reported by Masserman (10) and has been confirmed in a similar but simpler situation by Bailey and Miller (1). They found that an injection of sodium amytal caused cats in a simple approach-avoidance conflict to resume eating at the place where they had received electric shocks.

Extension to psychotherapy. A still further extension of the model to cover some of the phenomena observed in psychotherapy has been made by Dollard and Miller (6). This extension involves the following additions to the partial definitions:

(A) The definition of *nearness* is extended to apply to any situation in which the subject can be said to be coming nearer to a goal in space, time, or some dimension of qualitative or culturally defined similarity of cues.

(B) The definition of *avoidance* is extended to apply to the responses producing inhibition and repression.

(C) The definition of *approach* is extended to apply to the responses that are inhibited or repressed.

It is obvious that it will be more difficult to secure complete agreement on the application of these definitions to clinical phenomena than it was to secure agreement on the application of the preceding ones to simple experimental situations. Probably we will have to make a number of additional, more exact definitions (involving the construction of various scales) before we can achieve complete agreement and more adequately test these applications of the model. Furthermore, it is quite possible that the foregoing definitions are too broad; for example, the gradients of all responses now classified as avoidance may not fall off more steeply than all of those now classified as approach. Perhaps a different type of classification, based on the nature of the motivation involved, may be found to fit the empirical facts better.

Nevertheless, as a first approximation, a number of significant deductions seem to be fairly well confirmed by the clinical observations that are available. Going part way and then stopping, or in other words, being unable to achieve or leave the goal, seems to be characteristic of patients in an approach-avoidance conflict. Furthermore, weakening the strength of the drive motivating avoidance or increasing the strength of the drive motivating approach seems to cause patients to go nearer to the goal.

At this point we come to some new deductions which may be made with the help of an additional basic assumption, namely, that the *strength of fear elicited* at any given distance from a feared stimulus is a function of the height of the avoidance gradient at that point. Turning back to Figures 1 and 2, the following relationships can be seen to hold for the range of changes within which the two gradients intersect:

(A) Increasing the strength of approach causes the subject to go nearer to the feared goal, and at this point stronger fear is elicited.

(B) Decreasing the over-all strength of avoidance causes the subject to go nearer to the goal, and at this point stronger fear is elicited.

(C) The increase in fear is greater when the same distance of approach toward the goal is produced by raising the gradient of approach than when it is produced by lowering the gradient of avoidance. (It will be noted that this deduction is dependent on the fact that the gradient of avoidance is steeper than that of approach.)

(D) In each of the above cases greater distances of approach toward the goal should produce greater increases in fear. (In order not to be dependent upon the assumption of linearity, this deduction must be restricted to those cases in which the greater distance of approach includes the smaller one.)

(E) After the goal is reached, further increases in the strength of approach should not produce further increases in the fear elicited, and further reductions in the strength of avoidance should produce reductions in the fear elicited.

The evidence supporting these deductions has been summarized in somewhat more detail elsewhere (6); it can only be suggested here. The first of these deductions is in line with the clinical evidence that increasing the patient's motivation to approach seems to increase his fear and conflict. As would be expected from the fourth and fifth deductions, such increases are practicable without producing intolerable fear only when the patients are relatively near to the goal, either because the initial conflicts are weak or because they are approaching the end of successful therapy. These increases do not seem to be practicable in the face of the strong inhibitions and repressions of the severe neurotic.

The second deduction offers an explanation for the paradoxical negative therapeutic effect. After the therapist has succeeded in diminishing the patient's exaggerated idea of the dangerousness of the goal, he frequently observes an increase in the amount of fear and conflict elicited. Even more striking results appear where the conditions are better known and more clear-cut, namely, in the use of the barbiturates to treat amnesia produced by traumatic conditions of combat (6). In such cases the drug produces a marked decrease in the repression producing the amnesia for the traumatic events. This is what would be expected from the hypothesis we have already discussed—that this drug reduces the fear motivating avoidance. But, as the amnesia is lifted and the subject approaches nearer the goal of recovering his memory of the traumatic incidents, one observes an obvious increase in the amount of fear elicited. This is what would be expected from the deduction of the negative therapeutic effect.

The third deduction seems to be confirmed by the general experience of therapists that it is much better to concentrate on reducing avoidance (in other words, analyzing resistance) than on trying to increase approach. As would be expected from deductions (d) and (e), this is especially true during the early stages of the treatment of severe neurotics.

Generality of basic assumptions. One of the characteristics of a good model is that the same assumption is useful in a number of different deductions. Furthermore, it is often possible to integrate good models into a larger system. The first two basic assumptions, the gradients of approach and avoidance, can also be used to explain a number of the characteristics of avoidance-avoidance conflict and the difference between it and pure approach-approach competition (6, 11). It is obvious that these two assumptions are also used to explain a variety of phenomena in learning. They may be special cases of the gradient of reinforcement, which itself may turn out to be deducible from stimulus generalization and learned reinforcement (18).

It will be noted that the third basic assumption, greater steepness of avoidance, is essential to the explanation of three quite independent types of fact: the results of the separate measures of approach and avoidance by the strength-of-pull technique, the behavior of going part way and then stopping, and the greater therapeutic effectiveness of reducing the motivation for avoidance by analyzing resistance instead of attempting to increase the strength of approach.

As has been shown elsewhere (6), the fourth basic assumption, the effect of drive on the over-all height of the gradient, seems also to be useful as a possible explanation for the effect of motivation on perceptual responses. The fifth basic assumption, that the strongest response will occur, is a general one in stimulus-response theory (9).

Finally, let us return to the third basic assumption, the greater steepness of avoidance than approach. It is possible to deduce this (at least in the simple experimental situation in which approach is motivated by hunger and avoidance by fear) from the notions of response-produced drive and stimulus generalization (12). Since fear is a learned drive, it will be most strongly aroused by the cues originally most closely associated with reinforcement. Therefore, when the subject is confronted with cues at a distance, or a stimulus situation somewhat different from the original one, the gradient of stimulus generalization will have a double effect—it will weaken not only the specific responses involved in withdrawal, but also the fear motivating these responses. This double effect will cause the avoidance to fall off rapidly. On the other hand, since the hunger drive motivating approach is a primary one, more nearly dependent on internal physiological factors, it will be less influenced by the changes in cues so that its strength will remain relatively constant. The factor of generalization will operate only on the approach habit; it will not also affect the drive. Therefore, the gradient of approach should fall off less steeply than that of avoidance.

A simple deduction from this analysis has been experimentally tested by Miller and Murray (15). One group of rats learned an avoidance habit with a strong electric shock and were tested without shock so that they were motivated only by the learned drive of fear. Another group of rats were trained with a weaker shock and tested with shock so that they were motivated by the primary drive of pain. (The difference in the strengths of the training shocks was introduced only to keep the test responses of the two groups at the same general level.) When tested in the original learning situation, the first group pulled harder than the second; when tested for stimulus generalization in a different situation, the second pulled harder than the first. This confirms the deduction that a response motivated by a learned drive should be weakened more by stimulus generalization than one motivated by a primary drive. It provides a possible link between this model of conflict behavior and Miller's (13) theory of learnable drives and rewards.

REFERENCES

1. BAILEY, C. J., AND MILLER, N. E. Effect of sodium amytal on behavior of cats in an approach-avoidance conflict. *J. comp. physiol. Psychol.* To appear.
2. BROWN, J. S. The generalization of approach responses as a function of stimulus intensity and strength of motivation. *J. comp. Psychol.*, 1942, **33**, 209-226.
3. BROWN, J. S. Gradients of approach and avoidance responses and their relation to level of motivation. *J. comp. physiol. Psychol.*, 1948, **41**, 450-465.
4. CARNAP, R. Testability and meaning. *Phil. Sci.*, 1936, **3**, 420-471.
5. CONGER, J. J. The effects of alcohol on conflict behavior in the albino rat. *Quart. J. Stud. Alcohol.*, 1951, **12**, 1-29.
6. DOLLARD, J., AND MILLER, N. E. *Personality and psychotherapy.* New York: McGraw-Hill, 1950.
7. FEIGL, H. Some remarks on the meaning of scientific explanation. In H. Feigl and W. Sellars (eds.), *Readings in philosophical analysis.* New York: Appleton-Century-Crofts, 1949. Pp. 510-514.
8. HEMPEL, C. G. The function of general laws in history. In H. Feigl and W. Sellars (eds.), *Readings in philosophical analysis.* New York: Appleton-Century-Crofts, 1949. Pp. 459-471.
9. HULL, C. L. *Principles of behavior.* New York: Appleton-Century-Crofts, 1943.
10. MASSERMAN, J. H. *Behavior and neurosis.* Chicago: Univ. of Chicago Press, 1943.

11. MILLER, N. E. Experimental studies of conflict. In J. McV. Hunt (ed.), *Personality and the behavior disorders.* New York: Ronald, 1944. Pp. 431-465.

12. MILLER, N. E. Theory and experiment relating psychoanalytic displacement to stimulus response generalization. *J. abnorm. soc. Psychol.,* 1948, **43**, 155-178.

13. MILLER, N. E. Learnable drives and rewards. In S. Stevens (ed.), *Handbook of experimental psychology.* New York: Wiley, 1951. Pp. 435-472.

14. MILLER, N. E., AND KRAELING, DORIS. Displacement: greater generalization of approach than avoidance in a generalized approach-avoidance conflict. *J. exp. Psychol.* To appear.

15. MILLER, N. E., AND MURRAY, E. J. Conflict and displacement: learnable drive as a basis for the steeper gradient of avoidance than of approach. *J. exp. Psychol.* To appear.

16. MURRAY, E. J., AND MILLER, N. E. Displacement: steeper gradient of generalization of avoidance than of approach with age of habit controlled. *J. exp. Psychol.* To appear.

17. SMYTH, H. D. From X-rays to nuclear fission. *Amer. Scient.,* 1947, **35**, 485-501.

18. SPENCE, K. W. The role of secondary reinforcement in delayed reward learning. *Psychol. Rev.,* 1947, **54**, 1-8.

19. STEVENS, S. S. Psychology and the science of science. *Psychol. Bull.,* 1939, **36**, 221-263.

20. WHITING, J. W. M., AND SEARS, R. R. Projection and displacement in doll play. Mimeographed manuscript. Laboratory of Human Development, Cambridge, Mass., 1949.

The Organization of Personality

H. J. EYSENCK

*Department of Psychology, Institute of Psychiatry
(Maudsley Hospital), University of London*

SCIENCE, as ordinarily understood, attempts to discover general rules or laws under which individual events can be subsumed. It attempts to describe the multiform world of experience through the formulation of abstract laws and the creation of abstract categories. This process of abstraction is absolutely fundamental to science; without abstraction there can be nothing but observation of particular occurrences. But "science is not interested in the unique event; the unique belongs to history, not to science." As Whitehead puts it,

the paradox is now fully established that the utmost abstractions are the true weapon with which to control our thought of concrete fact. To be abstract is to transcend particular concrete occasions of actual happenings. The construction with which the scientist ends has the neatness and orderliness that is quite unlike the varied and multiform world of common sense, yet, since science grows out of and returns to the world of common sense, there must be a precise connection between the neat, trim, tidy, exact world, which is the goal of science, and the untidy, fragmentary world of common sense.

If, then, we would construct a science of personality, we must seek for abstract models, concepts, mathematical functions, or what have you, which will adequately represent our knowledge—meager though it be—of existing facts, and which at the same time will point forward to new facts which can verify, modify, or refute our theoretical model. What are the main facts regarding personality which must be incorporated in such a model? I believe that a rough and ready answer at least can be given to these two questions, and that this answer must be phrased in terms of factorial analysis.

We find most of the main elements which our model must contain in Allport's well-known definition of personality as the "dynamic organization within the individual of those psychophysical systems that determine his unique adjustment to his environment"

(1). A brief discussion of these terms (differing in several important ways from Allport's) may be helpful in discovering just what it is that our model is required to represent.

(A) In the first place, we have to deal with an individual's adjustment (or failure to adjust) to his environment. In other words, our universe of discourse is *human behavior,* taking this term in its broadest sense as including speech (vocal and subvocal), movement, hormonal and autonomic changes, alpha rhythms, and indeed all *objectively recordable modifications of the environment.* This interpretation is in essence identical with Wolfle's "fundamental principle of personality measurement": "An individual reveals his own personality through any change he makes upon any type of material" (26).

(B) But clearly such an omnibus definition is not sufficient; it does not allow for differences in importance between different items of behavior. It is a fact that person A complains about hammer toes, that person B has hallucinations, that person C has invented a new and revolutionary scientific theory, that person D has stomach ulcers and suffers from autonomic imbalance, and that person E can ride a bicycle. But these facts are not equal in importance; some are clearly peripheral, others are more central in their import. Personality implies the organization of behavioral items into some kind of hierarchy, a hierarchy which determines the importance of any given item of behavior by reference to the system of relations obtaining between this item and all others.

(C) It is difficult to speak about the organization of behavioral acts; it is more usual to postulate certain psychophysical systems (instincts, drives, needs, traits, habits, attitudes, complexes, sentiments, etc.) which are believed to underlie the behavioral acts, and to apply the concept of organization to these abstractions. This is of course perfectly permissible, and indeed quite essential in any scientific discussion, provided the connection between observed behavior and hypothesized abstract concept is operationally defined and experimentally verifiable. Many concepts in common use— Freudian ones in particular—lack such definition, and cannot therefore justifiably be incorporated into what purports to be a scientific system of personality.[1]

(D) Our defintion so far gives only a cross-sectional picture at any one moment of time; clearly personality as conceived in this definition

---

[1] By this I do not mean to say that the hypotheses implied in terms like "transference," "catharsis," "narcissism," "anal and oral types," and "regression" are necessarily false. I believe that some are true and others false, but clearly my belief is irrelevant to science; science demands proof, not conviction or belief, and no acceptable proof has been forthcoming so far to substantiate the claims of the psychoanalytic school. A purist might even maintain, with some show of justice, that a concept or hypothesis which had no operational reference could not be regarded as "true" or "false," but merely as "meaningless." While much of modern "dynamic" theory would indeed appear to be nothing but such meaningless semantic manipulation of terms having no factual reference, it would hardly be reasonable to dismiss the whole Freudian point of view in this cavalier fashion. The difficulty appears to lie mainly in finding some agreement between psychoanalysts and psychologists as to the precise nature of the "factual referents" required.

would be a term of very limited usefulness if the organization of behavior implied in it were only temporary, and had no predictive value. Hence the term "determine" in Allport's definition; personality is conceived of as an enduring (though not necessarily unchanging) organization which enables us to make predictions regarding future behavior. As Cattell puts it, "the personality of an individual is that which enables us to predict what he will do in a given situation" (3).

Let us now attempt to construct a model of personality thus conceived which embodies various requirements. Figure 1 represents such an attempt. There are four main levels of organization which are recognizable in this structure. At the lowest level we have specific acts of behavior, or specific responses, labeled $S.R._1$, $S.R._2$, $S.R._3$, ... $S.R._n$. These are items of behavior, such as responses to experiences of everyday life, or to experimental tests, which are observed once, and may or may not be characteristic of the individual.

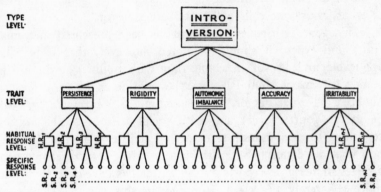

FIG. 1. Diagrammatic representation of hierarchical organization of personality.

At the second level, we have what are called habitual responses, $H.R._1$, $H.R._2$, $H.R._3$, ... $H.R._n$. These are specific responses which tend to recur under similar circumstances; i.e., if the test is repeated, a similar response is given, or if the life-situation recurs, the individual reacts in a similar fashion. This is the lowest level of organization; roughly speaking, the amount of organization present here can be measured in terms of reliability coefficients, i.e., in terms of the probability that on repetition of a situation behavior will be consistent.

At the third level, we have organizations of habitual acts into traits T_1, T_2, T_3, ... T_n. These traits—suggestibility, persistence, rigidity, irritability, accuracy, honesty, perseveration, fluency, or whatever the name may be—are theoretical constructs, based on observed intercorrelations of a number of different habitual responses; in the language of factor analysis they may be conceived of as group factors.

At the fourth level, we have organization of traits into a general *type;* in our example, the *introvert.* This is also based on observed intercorrelations, this time on correlations between the various traits which between them make up the concept of the type under discussion. Thus in our example persistence, rigidity, irritability, accuracy, autonomic imbalance, and various other traits would form a constellation of traits intercorrelating among themselves, thus giving rise to a higher-order construct, the type. This level, in factorial terminology, corresponds to a general factor, or to what Thurstone calls a "second order factor."[2]

This general four-level scheme has been presented in terms of traits and types; it should be noted, however, that it is equally applicable and useful in connection with abilities (where Thurstone's "Primary Mental Abilities" would lie at the third level, and his "Second-order Factor," corresponding to Spearman's "g," would lie at the fourth level) and with social attitudes. The argument regarding the hierarchical structure of abilities is presented by Vernon in some detail (25); with respect to the structure of attitudes a series of research reports by the writer has developed this concept more concretely (7, 9, 15, 16, 17). In this paper I shall confine myself, for the sake of brevity, to a discussion of traits and types, but exactly the same arguments can be applied to other areas of personality.

This general scheme obviously implies a methodology which will enable us to isolate the hypothetical third- and fourth-level

[2] There is in this scheme of course no assumption regarding the distribution of the population along the "trait" or "type" dimension. The stereotyped view that writers who have advocated typologies, like Jung and Kretchmer, conceive of the population as being distributed in a discontinuous, or at least bimodal, form of distribution, is not really in accord with the writings of these authors; it follows that much of the current criticism of typology based on this assumption falls to the ground. Indeed, it would be an elementary error in statistics to assume that the observed distribution of scores on a given test of extraversion-introversion, say, bore any necessary relation to the distribution of the underlying variable. Questions of distribution are meaningful only in terms of a specified metric, not in terms of raw scores on questionnaires of doubtful validity.

variables *uniquely* and *invariantly*. It is not sufficient, as Jung has done, to construct a system on the basis of observation and verbal material alone; at best this suffices to give us a hypothesis which permits of being tested empirically, but it does not provide us with such a test. Nor is it sufficient, as Kretschmer has done, to elaborate tests for the measurement of the various traits hypothesized, and to show that these discriminate significantly between criterion groups—schizophrenics and manic depressives, or leptosomatic and pyknic individuals (13). What is required is a method which enables us to apply rigid tests to questions implicit in the organizational scheme presented. This method can at the present be found only in the procedures of factor analysis. These procedures are of course too technical to be discussed here; however, certain methodological features implicit in them are so often misunderstood, by opponents as well as by many practitioners, that it may be worth while to state them explicitly.

Statistical analysis, as Kendall (19) has pointed out, can be of two main kinds—analysis of *dependence*, and analysis of *interdependence*. "In the latter we are interested in how a group of variates are related among themselves, no one being marked out by the conditions of the problem as of greater prior importance than the others, whereas in the analysis of dependence we are interested in how a certain specified group (the dependent variates) depend on the others." Analysis of variance and covariance, regression and confluence analysis are examples of the former; correlational analysis, component and factor analysis are examples of the latter. The general problem of component analysis is a simple one. Given a set of observations n on each variate of a p-variate complex, that is to say, given the array of values x_{ij}, $i=1, \ldots p$; $j=1, \ldots n$, can we (a) find new variables linearly connected with the old but fewer in number which will account for the original variation, and (b) if so, what are the new variables?

Various solutions to this problem are possible, most of them being approximations to the "principal components" solution. It has, in psychology, nearly always been found possible to find new variables fewer in number than the original variation within the limits of the sampling error; the question has usually been to decide which of an infinite set of such variables to accept. Of the methods proposed to decide on this question, the best known is undoubtedly Thurstone's method of "simple structure." As this method does not seem to lead to easily acceptable solutions in the noncognitive field, the writer has proposed a rather different method, that of "criterion analysis," which appears to lead to useful results in the field of temperament, character, social attitudes, and other noncognitive areas (10).

The apparent arbitrariness with which the particular set of variables constituting a solution to the general problem of interdependence analysis is chosen has offended many psychologists who feel that there should be one and only one right solution to problems of this kind. This view does not accord with experience in other scientific fields. As the problem of finding a small number of factors to represent a large number of observations is in many ways similar to that of finding physical dimensions to represent the multiform events of physics, we may perhaps quote briefly what physicists have to say about this problem. Thus, for instance, Bridgman declares: "There is nothing absolute about dimensions— they may be anything consistent with a set of definitions which agree with the experimental facts." Or we may take the discussion of the specific case of temperature, about which there has been much discussion in physics. Temperature "is sometimes taken as an independent primary quantity (H) so that such entities as specific heat and entropy will have dimensions including (H), viz. $L^2T^{-2}(H)^{-1}$ and $ML^2T^{-2}(H)^{-1}$ respectively. The situation becomes very much simplified, however, if, in the equations relating the pressure of a gas (p) to its specific volume (volume per unit mass v) and absolute temperature (T): $pv=RT$, we define the constant R as a dimensionless number. This gives T the dimensions $[ML^{-1}T^{-2}]$ x $[M^{-1}L^3]=L^2T^{-2}$ (an energy per unit mass) which leads to much simpler dimensions for specific heat (dimensionless) and entropy (M)" (24). Porter (23) goes so far as to say that this procedure "reveals the real dimensions of (H)." Scott Blair (24) comments on this that rather than revealing the real dimensions of (H) this procedure gives us a more convenient and effective way of expressing its dimensions and also those of a number of other entities involving temperature.

However we look at scientific concepts and models, it must be clear that dimensions and factors are not chosen by any absolute standards, but according to principles determined in their turn by usefulness, expediency, and other considerations intrinsic in the purposes of the scientist, rather than in his material. To condemn factor analysis because of a lack of "absolute" truth would mean to condemn the scientific method altogether. We may reword Bridgman's dictum slightly and say: There is nothing absolute about factors—they may be anything consistent with a set of definitions which agree with the experimental facts. The sting of this sentence is in the tail; when any considerable number of facts is known in a given field, it is usually difficult enough to find *one* set of dimensions of factors consistent with a set of definitions *and* agreeing with the experimental facts—there is seldom any opportunity to worry about the choice between a number of alternative sets of dimensions or factors. The fact that Spearman and Thurstone, starting out from very different premises, and using widely different methods, finally arrived at results which are in very good agreement illustrates this strong "determining tendency" exerted by the facts to perfection. Where there is still room for controversy, appeal to further facts still to be unearthed remains as always the only answer, and in so far as factor analysis leads to such further experimentation, it must be adjudged a fruitful and useful scientific method.

What is meant by such further experimentation may be briefly indicated by two examples. Having isolated the two factors of neuroticism and introversion-extraversion by factorial methods, and having constructed objective tests for the measurement of these dimensions (8), we attempted to apply these concepts to the study of the aftereffects of prefrontal lobotomy. The hypotheses investigated were based on the view that a factor denotes some underlying unitary personality process, and that a change in this process should be manifested in responses to all the tests used to define and measure that factor. The following hypotheses were formally set up and investigated:

(A) Lobotomy in patients suffering from neurotic illnesses leads to a shift on the neuroticism continuum towards the more normal end.

(B) Lobotomy in neurotic patients leads to a shift from the introverted towards the extraverted end on the introversion-extraversion continuum.

(C) The same shifts, but in a much attenuated form, would be expected to occur in psychotic patients.

Investigations by Petrie (20, 21, 22) of neurotic and Crown (5, 6) of psychotic patients have lent strong support to all these hypotheses.

Another hypothesis arose from the consideration that neuroticism is often believed to be an inherited predisposition, and that evidence regarding this proposition could be obtained by experimental studies on monozygotic and dizygotic twins. These studies, dealing with the inheritance of a *factor* rather than with the influence of heredity on the variance of a single test, have indeed shown that it is the factor *as a whole* which is inherited, thus disproving the view that a factor is nothing but a mathematical artifact (12). Other examples could be given of this tendency of factorial work to lead on to further experimentation, but these two must suffice for the present.

Many other objections are often brought forward against factor analysis, but these usually rest on a mistaken view of what the essential implications of this method really are. Another group of objections relates to specific findings; thus it may be said that a certain investigator discovered a certain cluster containing "the following hodge-podge: special acuities and pulchritude, combined with drive, but having some negative relation to empathy and to spatial facility" (1). Such objections are usually well founded as far as the specific example goes; they are obviously irrelevant as far as the usefulness of the method itself is concerned. Factor analysis is not a sausage machine into which any amount of rubbish can be thrown in the hope that ultimately meaningful results will emerge. Like all other mathematical tools, it demands a high degree of scientific competence and a thorough comprehension of the general problem before it can be used to advantage. That some of its devotees fall lamentably short of this ideal no one would deny; that their mistakes and failures should be used to discredit the method itself is hardly reasonable.

One set of objections occurs so frequently and has grown so much in volume in recent years that a few lines at least must be devoted to it. Factorial methods, it is said, leave out of account the fact that an individual's personality is something unique, something that cannot be analyzed into small pieces, is indeed an organismic whole which must be studied as such. This idiographic view—to use a term suggested by Windelband—has a certain appeal for most psychologists who have to deal with people because its main proposition is so obviously true. It is quite undeniably true that Professor Windelband is absolutely unique. So is my old shoe. Indeed, any existing object is unique in the sense that it is unlike any other object. This is true as much in the physical sciences as it is in the biological, sociological, and psychological sciences. But what precisely is this uniqueness? To some, it appears to be some mystical quality, something *sui generis,* distinguishing qualitatively between any two individuals. To the scientist, on the other hand, the *unique individual is simply the point of intersection of* a number of quantitative variables. There are some 340,000 discriminable color experiences, each of which is absolutely unique and distinguishable from any other. From the point of view of descriptive science, however, they can all be considered as points of intersection of three quantitative variables, hue, tint, and chroma. A combination of perfectly general, descriptive variables is sufficient to enable any individual to be differentiated from any other through specification of his position on each of these variables in a quantitative form. Many writers "seem unable to see that one individual can differ quantitatively from another in many variables, common variables though they may be, and still have a unique personality" (1). Quite on the contrary, the very notion of "being different from" implies at the same time the idea of direction and the idea of amount— in other words, two unique individuals cannot meaningfully be said to be different from each other unless they are being compared along some quantitative variable. Uniqueness, therefore, is not in any sense a concept antagonistic to science; it follows from the methods used in science to describe individual events in terms of common variables.

The second claim made by the idiographically minded is related to the necessity of studying individuals as wholes, rather than by means of any analytic method. A brief investigation of the methods used by those who favor such a "global" study will reveal that their procedure is hardly commensurate with their claims. A new nomenclature does not disguise the fact that the same "analytic" concepts have been taken over into this vaunted "study of the whole personality." To take but two examples: The Rorschach supposedly is able to diagnose a patient's "intellectual level," his "degree of maturity," his "creative or imaginative capacities," his "degree of control," and many other traits or abilities taken over directly from the workshop of the "nomothetic" psychologist. The Thematic Apperception Test is scored in terms of "Need" and "Press," a veritable palimpsest in which the original writing of McDougall, Shand, and a host of hoary Scottish philosophers is still plainly visible. It is difficult to see any great difference in these new "total" methods, unless it be that reliabilities are usually low, validities are assumed rather than demonstrated, and justification is in terms of philosophical argument rather than of empirical demonstration. It is plainly impossible to study the "whole personality" all at once, just as it is impossible to study the "whole universe"; parts of "sub-wholes" have to be analyzed out of the total complex of features and studied separately. Only when this task has been completed can we hope to study the interaction, organization, or structure of these parts. The organization of personality is not an act of faith; it is an object of empirical study.

In spite of their inconclusive nature, the objections raised by the idiographically minded do face us with a problem which factor analysts have not always considered with sufficient care. We have a model of personality, as it were, which determines our hypotheses; we have a method of analysis which we believe capable of providing us with the required proof; but what of the data needed before we can use this powerful method? Clearly, no method is capable of improving on data which are themselves worthless; yet psychologists have often carried out refined statistical procedures on data whose reliability and validity were more than doubtful. In general, I believe that certain types of data are unlikely to give results of sufficient accuracy to vouchsafe the laborious analyses required by the factorial approach; I do not believe that questionnaires or ratings are likely to provide the evidence which we require to construct an objective science of personality. Admittedly, data are easily gathered in this fashion; however, this ease of collection would appear to be inversely related to their psychological value. Cattell's work (3) is partly vitiated by this reliance on ratings; however, his awareness of the necessity to provide more objective data and to link them with the factors isolated from the analysis of ratings shows a promise that in due course we will understand better than we do now the complex interactions between rater and rates which form the basis of so many analyses (4). In any case, Cattell has attempted to forestall criticism by careful consideration of the categories to be rated. Other writers, however, have been less aware of the pitfalls involved in this type of work, and have used categories which can hardly be considered to represent modern thought. Burt's (2) analyses of ratings carried out in terms of McDougall's scheme of instincts lose most of their psychological interest through this use of an outmoded theory, and must be regarded more as exercises in statistical theory than as contributions to psychological knowledge.

The only type of data which in my view is likely to give trustworthy results is what I have called "objective performance tests." Elsewhere I have discussed at length possible classifications of psychological tests, the respective strengths and weaknesses of questionnaires, of so-called projective methods, of psychometric tests, and of the various other types which can be distinguished. If I may quote briefly:

There is one tentative generalization which, while it cannot be regarded as firmly established, may yet provide an heuristic hypothesis to serve as a basis for structuring the very confused field of modern psychological tests. It is widely agreed that personality rests on a firm hereditary basis, but is also subject to great alterations through social and other environmental influences. It would appear, by and large, that personality tests of the objective performance type are related rather more closely to the inherited pattern of a person's conative and affective traits; tests of conditioning, of suggestibility, of autonomic imbalance, of sensory dysfunctioning and of motor expression appear so closely bound up with the structural properties of the nervous system and with the body build and the sensory equipment of a person that the likelihood of hereditary determination can hardly be gainsaid. On the other hand, tests employing unstructured material would appear to reflect more the historical aspects of a person's life history and be subject to day-to-day fluctuations of mood and outlook. If we may use an analogy from physics we might say that tests of this type deal with problems of hysteresis rather than with those of structure. (11)

Evidence for this proposition will be found in the article from which this brief summary has been quoted and in several experimental studies reported elsewhere (8, 12, 14). They all lend support to the view that objective performance tests are more likely than any other type to provide the required data for our purposes.

When we come to the application in practice of the scheme outlined here, and of the method discussed, we find that there are two main ways of proceeding. We may start with a *tabula rasa,* as it were, and attempt to encompass the whole "personality sphere" in our analysis. This, roughly, is what Cattell has attempted in a series of studies published over the past six years or so. Or we may take existing theories regarding personality organization, such as Jung's theory of extraversion-introversion, or Kretschmer's theory of schizothymia-cyclothymia, and devise experimental and statistical tests to see whether deductions made from these theories can be verified. This is the method the present writer has followed in the main. In the long run, both methods should be expected to give identical results, and already marked similarities are beginning to emerge where the territory covered has overlapped at all.

The method advocated here may be illustrated by means of a concrete problem, viz. that of psychiatric diagnosis. If we confine ourselves for the moment to the main classifications, "neurosis" and "psychosis," we find the following distinct theories, all of which are explicitly or implicitly held by large numbers of psychiatrists and psychoanalysts.

(A) The two classes represent one general dimension of "psychosexual regression," so that the psychotic has regressed most, the neurotic much less, and the normal, who presumably forms the pole opposite to the psychotic, not at all. We thus postulate a single continuum ranging from normal through neurotic to psychotic.

(B) Neurosis and psychosis are separate and distinct disease-processes, quite independent one of the other; both are conceived as quantitative variables continuous with the normal, and representing extremes of their respective variates.

(C) Mental disorders are qualitatively different from normal mental states, and therefore something *sui generis,* discontinuous with normality. This would be the view of those psychiatrists who believe in the genetic determination of mental disease through one or two distinct genes (as opposed to the multi-factorial theory of inheritance).

In practice, many psychiatrists will be found to hold not one of these views, but to combine points from all three, incompatible though they are, talking at one time in terms of one theory, at other times in terms of another. Even psychiatric textbooks usually fail to face squarely the problem thus presented, and adopt several contradictory theories at different stages of their discussion.

Two points are involved in this problem: (a) Continuity or discontinuity? (b) Do psychosis and neurosis constitute one or two dimensions? The method of "criterion analysis" was originally devised to answer the first of these two problems, and it has been shown that both neurosis (10) and psychosis (14) are continuous with normality. The second question has also received an answer in factorial terms: it appears that neurosis and psychosis constitute two separate dimensions (12). However, this problem can be attacked by means of procedures other than factor analysis, and as these other procedures permit of a test of significance which is more accurate than the customary approximations used in factor analysis, I will state the conclusion in nonfactorial terms.[3]

Four tests (tests M, N, O, P from the U. S. E. S. General Aptitude Test Battery) were given to fifty normals, fifty non-deteriorated psychotics, and fifty neurotics. The four scores were condensed into the two canonical variates that give the best discrimination of the three groups in two dimensions; the first variate, Y_1 and Y_2 were calculated, the latent roots were tested for significance, using Bartlett's test; both roots were significant at the $P=.001$ level. It follows from this that two dimensions are necessary and sufficient to account for the observed test data. Inspection of the scatter diagram shows that Y_1 carries the entire discrimination between normals and psychotics, and Y_2 discriminates between neurotics, and normals and psychotics. This result, therefore, strongly reinforces the conclusion derived from our factorial studies that neurosis and psychosis must be conceived as lying in two dimensions, not along one single dimension as posited by Freudians.

These results are important in two ways for the construction of an adequate model of personality. In the first place they lend experimental support, hitherto missing, to the frequent assumption that so-called abnormal, clinical cases of neurosis and psychosis can be used to furnish a guide to the structure of normal personality. This is permissible only on the assumption of *continuity,* and the proof that such continuity exists supplies an essential basis to the

[3] The analysis to be described was performed by A. Lubin, Senior Statistician in the Psychology Laboratory (19a). For the conclusions drawn I am myself responsible.

theories of Jung, Kretschmer, and others who make the abnormal field their point of departure.

In the second place, we now have the beginnings of a rational system of psychiatric diagnosis. Patients can be diagnosed as neurotic *or* psychotic only on the basis of an assumption of qualitative, noncontinuous differences. But if our results give an accurate picture of reality, the question "Is this patient neurotic or psychotic?" becomes as unreasonable as the question "Is this patient intelligent or tall?" Two orthogonal vectors, like neuroticism and psychoticism, generate a plane on which the position of an individual has to be indicated by reference to *both* vectors; we can only describe an individual by giving both his I. Q. and his height, or by giving both his degree of neuroticism and of psychoticism. This is illustrated in Figure 2. The ordinate and the abscissa respectively represent the factors neuroticism and psychoticism; the average person, in each case, is assumed to lie roughly at the center of these two variates. Representing an individual's position in two-dimensional space, therefore, position A would indicate the average person's standing, P would indicate the position of the average psychotic, N that of the average neurotic, and P + N that of a person suffering from both a neurotic and a psychotic illness. All other positions on the plane thus generated are possible locations for a given individual, and it will be seen that *mixed cases* are more likely than *pure cases*—we are more likely to find individuals in the plane of the diagram than on the ordinate or on the abscissa. This preponderance of mixed cases of course agrees well with clinical experience. Diagnosis, on this showing, should consist in the accurate determination of an individual's position on the plane, rather than, as is now usual, in a simple either-or judgment.

The picture is of course much more complicated than this. In addition to the two factors depicted in the diagram, we have many others which presumably play their part in determining the nature of the illness. The only one of these to be operationally defined in terms of objective tests is extraversion-introversion (8). Thus the person who is high on neuroticism and introversion would be seen clinically as a patient suffering from dysthymic disorders (anxiety, reactive depression, obsessional features); the person who is high on neuroticism and extraversion would be seen clinically as a pa-

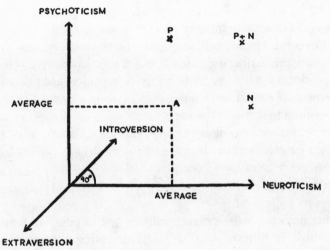

FIG. 2. Diagrammatic representation of three dimensions: psychoticism, neuroticism, introversion—extraversion.

tient suffering from hysterical (or possible psychopathic) symptoms. Schizothymia-cyclothymia is another possible dimension, although experimental work here has not yet proceeded far enough to isolate it, or to indicate its relation to the other dimensions described (14). The possibilities are, roughly, these: (a) Schizothymia-cyclothymia as a dimension may not exist at all; (b) it may coincide with extraversion-introversion, the extraverted psychotic showing manic-depressive symptoms; (c) it may exist as a separate dimension, in which case it would of course have projections on the other dimensions already isolated; (d) it may coincide with the psychotic dimension, indicating merely different degrees of severity of the illness. These hypotheses must of course be tested systematically before we can know how to incorporate schizothymia-cyclothymia into our model.

It is not hypothesized that these are the only dimensions into which personality can be analyzed, and along which measurement should take place; to take but one example, there is the case of intelligence (operationally defined in terms of Thurstone's second-order factor), which is more or less orthogonal to all the dimensions so far discussed. In due course, other dimensions will no doubt be isolated and measured, and much prospecting has already been done by Cattell (3) into possible lines of progress. But regardless of the actual number of independent dimensions which our picture of personality may require, it is clear that categorical diagnoses of the "either-or" kind are not warranted by the experimental findings; what is required is a separate assessment and measurement of each dimension in turn. It is not claimed that more than a beginning has been made in this complex, time-consuming, and difficult proceeding; it is believed, however, that results to date are fully in agreement with the general model of personality on which our procedures have been predicted.

SUMMARY

A hierarchical model of personality organization has been presented which is believed capable of representing the majority of experimentally determined facts regarding personality structure. The method of factorial analysis, with particular stress on the method of "criterion analysis," has been suggested to be best suited to help in the solution of the problems which arise in relating experimental facts to this model. A number of criticisms of the factorial method have been discussed, and its relation to concepts like "uniqueness" and "wholeness" has been clarified. Lastly, an example has been given of the application of the theoretical concepts and practical methods advocated here to the problem of psychiatric diagnosis.

REFERENCES

1. ALLPORT, G. W. Personality: a psychological interpretation. New York: Henry Holt, 1937.
2. BURT, C. The analysis of temperament. Brit. J. med. Psychol., 1937, 17, 158-188.
3. CATTELL, R. B. Description and measurement of personality. New York: World Book, 1946.
4. CATTELL, R. B., AND SAUNDERS, D. R. Inter-relation and matching of personality factors from behavior rating, questionnaire, and objective test data. J. soc. Psychol., 1950, 31, 243-260.
5. CROWN, S. An experimental study of psychological changes following prefrontal lobotomy. J. gen. Psychol. To appear.
6. CROWN, S. Psychological changes following prefrontal leucotomy. A review. J. ment. Sci. To appear.
7. EYSENCK, H. J. General social attitudes. J. soc. Psychol., 1944, 19, 207-227.
8. EYSENCK, H. J. Dimensions of personality. London: Kegan Paul, 1947.
9. EYSENCK, H. J. Primary social attitudes: I. The organization and measurement of social attitudes. Int. J. opin. & attit. Res., 1947, 1, 49-84.

10. EYSENCK, H. J. Criterion analysis—an application of the hypothetico-deductive method to factor analysis. *Psychol. Rev.*, 1950, **57**, 38-65.

11. EYSENCK, H. J. Personality tests: 1944-1949. In G. W. T. H. Fleming (ed.), *Recent progress in psychiatry*. London: Churchill, 1951.

12. EYSENCK, H. J. *The scientific study of personality*. London: Routledge, 1952.

13. EYSENCK, H. J. Cyclothymia-schizothymia as a dimension of personality. I. Historical. *J. Personal.*, 1950, **19**, 123-153.

14. EYSENCK, H. J. Cyclothymia-schizothymia as a dimension of personality. II. Experimental. *J. Personal.* To appear.

15. EYSENCK, H. J. Primary social attitudes and the "Social Insight" test. *Brit. J. Psychol.*, 1951, **40**, 114-122.

16. EYSENCK, H. J. Primary social attitudes as related to social class and political party. *J. Sociol.*, 1951, **2**, 198-209.

17. EYSENCK, H. J., AND CROWN, S. An experimental study in opinion-attitude methodology. *Int. J. opin. & attit. Res.*, 1949, **3**, 47-86.

18. GUILFORD, J. P. Unitary traits of personality and factor theory. *Amer. J. Psychol.*, 1936, **48**, 673-680.

19. KENDALL, M. G., AND SMITH, B. B. Factor analysis. *J. roy. stat. Soc.*, 1950, **12**, 60-94.

19ᵃ LUBIN, A. Some contributions to the testing of psychological hypotheses by means of statistical multivariate analysis. Ph.D. diss. Univ. London, 1951.

20. PETRIE, A. A preliminary report of changes after prefrontal leucotomy. *J. ment. Sci.*, 1949, **95**, 449-455.

21. PETRIE, A. Personality changes after prefrontal leucotomy. Report 2. *Brit. J. med. Psychol.*, 1949, **22**, 200-207.

22. PETRIE, A. Clinical aspects of leucotomy. *Proceed. roy. Soc. Med.*, 1950, **42**, 39.

23. PORTER, A. W. *The method of dimensions*. London: Methuen, 1933.

24. SCOTT-BLAIR, G. W. *Measurements of mind and matter*. London: Dennis Dobson, 1950.

25. VERNON, P. E. *The structure of human abilities*. London: Methuen, 1950.

26. WOLFLE, H. A fundamental principle of personality measurement. *Psychol. Rev.*, 1949, **56**, 273-276.

Biological Intelligence

WARD C. HALSTEAD

Departments of Medicine and Psychology, University of Chicago

PSYCHOLOGY appears to be divided today very much along the lines of a dichotomy perhaps unwittingly presaged by William James (20). In his *The Varieties of Religious Experience*, he wrote:

The first thing the intellect does with an object is to class it along with something else. But any object that is infinitely important to us . . . feels to us also as if it must be *sui generis* and unique. Probably a crab would be filled with a sense of personal outrage if it could hear us class it without ado or apology as a crustacean. "I am no such thing!" it would say, "I am Myself, Myself." (p. 171)

Hard-boiled classificationists or operationalists on the one hand and interpretative students of the individual on the other fill the scene of psychology today. Is it possible that the twain can meet? That the difficulties are great is more than suggested by the experiences of the late Robert Benchley. It is alleged, although not personally verified by this writer, that Benchley flunked his undergraduate economics at Harvard when he submitted a treatise *The Newfoundland Fishing Industry*, written from the point of view of the fish.

In the context of a symposium such as this, the operating "posture" of the author towards his subject matter should be made explicit at the outset. The present writer falls into the category of the operationalists. Furthermore, he finds himself heartily in sympathy with the efforts of Professor Murphy (23) to bring the problem of personality within the rubrics of general psychology:

Beneath all the limitless complexity of personal acts there is the general substratum, the system of organic potentialities—in short, the organism. This is approachable from many vantage points, by many techniques. When one combines several, and tries to see the whole organism at once, he may, if he wishes, say that he is studying personality. The organism the biologist studies and the personality the psychologist studies would be the same thing, except that the psychologist would tend to emphasize more complex functions, and more expressly indicate his desire to see all the interrelations within the organism at once, as well as the hierarchy of laws governing those interrelations. Psychology of personality would then be that particular kind of general psychology that emphasizes totality and the organic systematic relations which obtain within it. (p. 3)

Personalistic versus a general psychology. No psychologist would deny the aesthetic richness of, for example, Professor Allport's (1) psychology of personality, with its great emphasis on the self or individual.[1] Both the statics and dynamics of the individual constitute the propaedeutics of behavioral science. No real conflict of goals in psychology exists when personality is viewed in this perspective. The limiting consideration here may well be the nature of mental operations underlying science, which ultimately incorporates only the *rational* end-points of ego-activity, a kind of collective rationality. Science thus constitutes a smaller behavioral universe than that which produces it, for even scientists live and work not by rationality alone.

Concepts versus constructs. Concepts are the models through which we schematize or order the phenomena of a given domain for purposes of communication and continuing investigation. In terms of the idiom of science they are "good" concepts or models in so far as they transcend their particulars and advance the *level of adaptation*—general scientific understanding. They are "bad" concepts, although sometimes useful as constructs, when they remain secular or unincorporated into the mainstreams of scientific knowledge. Concepts are thus the engrams of science as opposed to the constructs of lesser generality found in particular scientific disciplines. In the history of chemistry, for example, phlogiston was a construct of temporary heuristic value in ordering the phenomena of combustion. Fortunately for biochemistry, it gave way to the concept of oxidation, which today orders relevant events of combustion throughout the physical and biological sciences.

The orderly growth or transition from constructs to concepts is probably no less a significant process in the "maturing" of an individual personality than in a particular science. Increasing levels of orientation and security in some respects appear to go hand in hand. As I write these sentences, seated now as on occasion then

[1] This statement applies no less to the personalistic psychology of William Stern (26), the holistic psychology of Kurt Lewin (22) and of Kurt Goldstein (10), and to the Freudian idiom (8, 21). A provocative study of six personalities from a personalistic point of view by Wilson (28) is currently, I believe, a Book-of-the-Month selection.

a mere hundred yards from the spot where man first brought forth a sustained nuclear fission reaction, I am of necessity impressed by the generality of the concepts which entered into those operations. This triumph of mind over matter provides evidence enough for the existence of that intelligence which the late Professor Thorndike (27) called "some unified, coherent, fundamental fact in the world."[2] An operational model for this "fundamental fact" will concern us in the following sections.

Biological intelligence. The contributions of Alfred Binet (7) to the problem of intelligence are known chiefly through the standardized test associated with his name. Less well known is the fact that Binet early in his investigations found it necessary to distinguish between intellectual *activity* and intellectual *level:*

Who has not encountered persons who busy themselves with a host of questions, have a great deal of information, speak of everything with warmth and an inexhaustible supply of words, are fertile in views, hypotheses, distinctions, neologisms? Very often they deceive as to their true value. They are thought very intelligent, while in reality they possess only intellectual activity.

Binet also emphasized the significance of intelligence as a form of biological adaptation: "One must remember that the faculty of adapting oneself is the property of the intelligence and that the power of adaptation is the measure of it; it is evident that from this point of view any confusion between the activity and the level is impossible" (p. 87).

Binet thus approached intelligence from the point of view of the biologically oriented psychologist. He recognized both genotypic and phenotypic components. There is little question but that he assigned the intellectual level to the former. As to the scale which Binet produced for measuring intelligence, and its subsequent modification by Terman, I suspect that it is a better measure of intellectual activity than of intellectual level. This, of course, is not the outcome which Binet had hoped for but, as Hebb (17) has convincingly demonstrated, the I. Q. may or may not be changed and may be normal for the scale with the major part of both frontal lobes (about 30 per cent of the cerebrum) absent.

---

[2] As an individual scientist and citizen I may express the hope that this concept may prove to have the same generality as those underlying nuclear fission.

Binet's reaction to this recent finding would, I am sure, have been to make better tests. His clinical insight was too keen to permit the easy inference—which unfortunately is being made rather commonly today—that the frontal brain has nothing to do with intelligence (16).

Binet's distinction between intellectual level and intellectual activity has largely been overlooked or forgotten by contemporary students of the problem. I would like to state parenthetically that if all other reasons were lacking, which they are not, the continuing need for parameters other than performance to aid in specifying level of behavioral organization[3] is sufficient to link the future destinies of psychology and basic biology. It seems that this need is also felt in the rapidly developing field of biochemistry (cf. Himwich, 19) where there appears to be a gross correlation at least between the demands in energy level and the corresponding levels of behavioral functions organized around particular areas of the brain.

During the last several years, while exploring the behavioral effects of surgical lesions in the frontal lobes of man and other animals, the writer (13) has identified certain recurrent forms of behavior which have their maximal though not exclusive representation in the cortex of the frontal lobes. Since it appeared that the functions thus isolated bore directly upon the capacity for controlled adaptability of the individuals involved, a concept of biological intelligence was generated. The adjective *biological* was appended when it became apparent that the functions were relatively independent of cultural considerations and had a wide generality.

Components of biological intelligence. Four factors have thus far been identified as comprising biological intelligence. They have been designated neutrally as A, P, C, and D factors respectively. Collectively they constitute a neural Gestalt which can be selectively impaired or enhanced by certain classes of stress such as anoxia, drugs, hypnotic inhibition,[4] trauma, and disease. They have now been scaled fairly satisfactorily in several hundred individuals, including males and females through the age range of 12 to 75, in

[3] A determination of blood alcohol level is very helpful in discriminating operationally among equivalent performances, some of which may simulate "drunkenness."

[4] Mr. Richard R. Willey: An experimental investigation of the attributes of hypnotizability. Unpublished doctoral dissertation, June, 1951. On file at the Department of Psychology, University of Chicago.

various stages of health and disease. The functions involved appear to mature sometime between 12 and 14 years of age. That they are relatively free from cultural considerations is further attested by their determined presence in Eskimos, Orientals, Negroes, and Caucasians. The functions are scalable with present indicators at a high level of objectivity. In recent test runs they have been satisfactorily scaled remotely, i.e., without any sensory contact between interpreter and subject. Each of the factors is correlated positively but to a low degree (r's of the order of .39) with both verbal and performance psychometric I. Q. That they project into the domain of personality is strongly suggested by positive correlations of the order of .70 between some of them and specific components of the Rorschach test.[5] What is the nature of these factors?

The A factor. Two components of the A factor have been identified in grouping behavior. Both are involved in grouping to a criterion. One yields rational outcome and to some extent involves conscious awareness. The other yields an irrational outcome without dependence upon awareness. Behavior of the first class can be demonstrated by means of the writer's Category Test. In this test groups of simple geometrical figures are presented serially to the subject in such a manner that he can infer recurrent principles of organization in the stimulus material. Information as to the quality of response for each given set of items is fed back differentially via the auditory system of the subject in the form of a chime registering correct responses and a buzzer registering incorrect responses. In a test situation where several principles of organization are made effective through the exposure of 200 or 300 sets of figures, the orderly transition from trial-and-error groping to formation of constructs of limited generality, to the generalization of concepts of high generality can be traced in a clear manner for the normal subject. In some fifteen years I have yet to find an individual from any walk of life with known damage to the cortex of his frontal lobes who has succeeded in making the orderly transition from constructs to concepts of wide generality. This test of organizational activity or abstraction, which healthy twelve- to

---

[5] Mr. Ralph M. Reitan: Relationships of certain Rorschach indicators to the abstraction and power factors of biological intelligence. Unpublished doctoral dissertation, December, 1950. On file at the Department of Psychology, University of Chicago.

fourteen-year-old children with average I. Q.'s can pass without difficulty, has proved sensitive throughout a wide range of conditions involving frontal brain injuries. It will not detect reliably primary brain lesions occurring elsewhere.

Perceptual difficulties cannot account for the failures since the subject is always able to describe the items in detail. Likewise, failure of brief memory seems to be ruled out by the performances on the last subtest, which is a recognition test. Our evidence suggests that the differences arise in direct proportion to the blindness of the task for the various subjects. At various times the normal subjects seem to ignore very obvious dimensions of the stimulus configurations. They usually begin the test by isolating some stimulus dimension which is sufficiently recurrent to produce temporary signs of successful performance. But when this initial cue proves to be but an incidental rather than a necessary element of the task, they may persist for several items in projecting their initial construct onto the materials before moving to generate a valid principle or concept. In this respect they appear to differ only quantitatively from the brain-injured individuals; yet this difference is all important. They do shift more readily to other aspects of the situation and hence discover the necessary and sufficient attributes among the ambient dimensions of the stimuli at a much earlier stage. Ordering of their behavior with reference to test stimuli is at once more conscious and insightful, involving active effort. But lest we consider these latter qualities characteristic of the normal individual, let us examine the second type of ordered behavior wherein the normal individual generalizes towards an irrational outcome as blindly as do our most severely brain-injured individuals.

Schematic faces and affective behavior. Some years ago Brunswik and Reiter (9) undertook an interesting study of certain physiognomic stereotypes in normal individuals. They employed ten judges. Using the method of paired comparisons they asked their individuals to match up certain personality traits with schematic outlines of faces. Out of several hundred comparisons, they were able to isolate a dozen or more relatively strong schematic faces which were commonly associated with personality traits. It occurred to me to apply such materials to the study of human brain-injured individuals. Professor Brunswik kindly made available to me photographic negatives of his originals. From these I selected nine faces for the purposes of my study (11, Fig. 212). Three of these faces had been found by Brunswik and Reiter and also by Samuels (25), working with Harvard students, to be strongly associated with such desirable personality traits as gaiety, good character, intelligence, beauty, youth, etc. Five of these faces, on the other hand, had been found to be strongly associated with such undesirable personality traits as sadness, ugliness, bad character, unintelligence, and old age. The other face, J9, was found to be psychophysically neutral, being chosen with equal frequency for desirable and undesirable traits. Over a period of several years we have had an opportunity to study the responses of several hundred individuals to the schematic faces presented to them by a modification of the method of limits.

The extent to which grouping behavior of the second type with reference to schematic faces occurs among our subjects is shown in Table I. Here the percentages of various subgroups who selected the schematic faces according to desirable (D) and undesirable (U) are shown for each of fourteen traits. Thus 86 per cent of our controls chose one of the expected three faces as the most gay, whereas chance would have yielded but 33.3 per cent. On the other hand, 95 per cent of them chose one of the expected five faces as being the most sad, whereas chance would have yielded but 55.6 per cent. Note also that our brain-injured cases and our severely neurotic patients matched gaiety and sadness in a very similar way. In fact, if we look at the various pairs of personality traits shown in this table, we are impressed by the striking similarities rather than by the differences in the grouping behavior. In this type of behavior, our normal individuals are just as irrational as our brain-injured individuals or as our psychiatric patients. It is difficult to see that such ordering behavior is on other than a blind basis. It seems quite unlikely that the child is born with an a priori notion that the distance between the eyes, the height of the forehead, the length of the nose, or the location of the mouth, the four varying elements in this series of faces, are invariable indicators of gaiety, intelligence, etc.

We are not clear when this process begins, but we have found one instance in which a child of four years and ten months required

TABLE I

PERCENTAGE OF AGREEMENT IN PROJECTING PERSONALITY TRAIT NAMES
ONTO SCHEMATIC FACES ACCORDING TO CATEGORIES OF DESIRABLE (D) AND
UNDESIRABLE (U) TRAITS, IN NORMAL-CONTROL, BRAIN-DISEASE, AND
MENTAL-ILLNESS SUBJECTS

Trait	SUBJECTS					
	Controls N=102		Brain Disease N=158		Mental Illness N=103	
	D	U	D	U	D	U
Gay	86		86		90	
Sad		95		92		87
Beautiful	92		92		80	
Ugly		92		91		93
Good Character	83		77		80	
Bad Character		76		81		76
Intelligent	68		77		73	
Unintelligent		89		82		84
Likable	86		86		84	
Unlikable		86		85		84
Young	90		87		91	
Old		89		86		89
Energy & Determination	60		64		56	
Lacks Energy & Determination		86		86		85

Chance expectancy: D=33.3%; U=55.6%

but slight translation of the trait names to show this conformity or stereotypy in thirteen of the fourteen judgments. This situation may not be fundamentally different from the irrational or blind learning that takes place when a newcomer begins to take on the dialect of the community or from the process of identification of the child with one or both of his parents.

It is this strong projective tendency to fix upon particular aspects which we noted to occur under the more restricted conditions of our Category Test. Herein lies a clue as to the nature of the type of abstraction or grouping behavior that yields an insightful grasp of principles. The organism works initially less directly with the external material than with its a priori expectancies. True categorization is achieved only when these expectancies have been put through a special set of operations in which a redistribution of affective loadings or valences takes place. The altered content must be rendered affectively equivalent. It is this type of work for which the organism is perhaps least prepared by its biological heritage. The task requires deliberation with denial of immediate gratifications. It requires that the organism be able to protect its state of deliberation in the face of mounting frustration. If the organism is to maintain deliberativeness in the face of mounting frustration, there must be an adequate reserve of power, cortical or intellectual, for, as much experimental work indicates, frustration per se does not add power to the task but rather is parasitic to it.

The P factor. One of our indicators appears to measure something which we interpret as cerebral power (12). We call this the P factor. It is measured with the simple task of adjusting the speed of a flickering light until the flicker disappears. This point represents a dramatic change in consciousness for the subject. For once he reaches the rate at which the separate flashes run together or fuse for him, he cannot tell the unsteady light from a steady one. He has broken with physical reality. This rate is much higher in our normal individuals than in our frontal brain-injured patients (13). It is as if the mental engine were running in the brain-injured, but running on inadequate power. It fails at the first little hill. From our measurements with this test under a considerable range of physiological conditions, it seems clear that the test reflects an important aspect of cerebral metabolism and possibly that of the cerebral cortex itself. For the power factor may not be lowered by the operation known as prefrontal lobotomy, wherein the deep white matter of the frontal lobes is destroyed by leaving the overlying cortex intact. Whereas it is lowered when the cortex is removed as in frontal lobectomies.

Support for our notion that we are measuring some aspect of cerebral metabolism has been obtained by studying patients with various types of metabolic disorders. Our endocrinologist, Dr. Allen Kenyon, has made many such cases available to us prior to and after treatment with various hormones (6). In patients with hypothyroidism or myxedema, for example, remarkable increases in the power factor occur as these individuals are placed on thyroid medication. In some instances, this change appears to reflect quite accurately a general improvement in the clinical status of the individual. Not only does the power factor increase but the ability of these patients to make the required adaptations to our Category Test likewise is improved—frequently to normal limits. ACTH likewise produces an increase in the power factor in some individuals. Other hormones, such as some of the estrogens, have failed in our experience to produce these effects.

The A factor, or capacity for abstracting universals or rational concepts, seems to be a general property of the cerebral cortex in man that is maximized in the cortex of the prefrontal lobes. The cerebral power factor P also seems to be represented throughout the cortex but again is maximized in the cortex of the prefrontal lobes. These two factors are disturbed together in unilateral or bilateral lobectomies of the frontal lobes wherein the cortex is removed along with the white matter. Both factors may be spared in lobotomies, however, wherein the white matter is destroyed leaving the frontal cortex essentially intact. On the other hand, spontaneous mild atrophy of the frontal cortex in middle-aged persons may first impair the A factor and only later as the atrophy progresses come to impair the P factor. Such individuals represent the obverse of clinical depressions. There may be no flagging of intellectual drive and ambition in the face of mounting judgmental incapacity. The mild clinical depression, probably as a direct function of the substrate, is associated with an acute drop in the P factor with only a more gradual restriction of the degrees of freedom for the A factor. If we restate the above in terms of Binet's distinction between *level* and *activity,* it is apparent that an individual may have high level in P and low activity in A, or vice versa, and all intermediate ratios of A and P. The possibility that psychotherapy, for example, is effective by changing the A factor and P factor ratios to a more "optimal" balance is a matter for future research.

The D factor. There is a third factor in our conception of biological intelligence which must be taken into account. This is the avenue or modality through which intelligence is exteriorized in any given situation. Our clue to the neural significance of the directional or D factor arises in studies of the aphasias. It is well known that an agnosia for printed words may so deform biological intelligence on the perceptual side that the affected individual may be able to transact his affairs by telephone but cannot read his mail (14). Or, conversely, an individual may have an apraxia for producing written symbols, and although he cannot write a single word be able to demonstrate in our tests that he is of normal intelligence.

In the early stages of any skill, the modality or avenue considerations may be the most important. You have to "get the feel" of a golf club before you can develop an intelligent game of golf. Some of the agnosias and apraxias seem to result from focal cortical lesions, according to Nielsen (24). The cortical representations of others are as yet unknown. But certainly an operational description of intelligence must include among its necessary and sufficient conditions provisions for our D factor.

The C factor. It is the fourth factor in biological intelligence which poses special difficulties in finding its neural correlates. The C factor, or organized experience of the individual, is the memory factor in intelligence. It serves as the stable framework of the "familiar" against which "new" experience is tested. A nervous system that cannot store its experience, that is, remember, is in trouble for the level of adaptation to new situations will necessarily be low. Trauma or disease of the brain, and excessive affect or emotion may disturb the memory component of intelligence. There is as yet no clue as to what these agents have in common. As to the physiology of learning, our ignorance is virtually complete. According to Hilgard (18) : "It is a blot upon our scientific ingenuity that after so many years of search we know as little as we do about the physiological accompaniments of learning." I would put the matter even more strongly and say that the physiology and biochemistry of learning are the missing keys to further understanding of certain functions of the brain. In support of this view, Dr. Joseph Katz, a chemist, and I have recently published a theory of the memory trace designed to elicit help from the biochemist on this formidable problem (15). We have suggested that the genetic apparatus is a recapitulation or memory device which is more than formally analogous to individual memories arising from human experience. We have presented arguments for the view that individual memory begins with the laying down of a template protein molecule similar to a gene. Like the gene, this template molecule then organizes available neural proteins into protein lattices which register the particular memory trace. New instruments and techniques for exploring the ultramicroscopic structures of the neural elements of the brain have recently been introduced. We must await their verdict on the ultimate nature of memory.

Theoretical extensions. Such then is a skeletal view of biological intelligence. Some of the possible biosocial extensions of the model are being examined currently with the help of clinical methods on the one hand (2, 3, 4, 5) and factor analyses on the other. There remains the task of testing the model against such concepts in general psychology as perception, emotion, motivation, learning, and thinking and against such related concepts as growth, maturation, homeostasis, and integration in general biology. As the above tasks approach various stages of completion, the writer grows in optimism concerning biological intelligence as an operational concept with scientific generality.

REFERENCES

1. ALLPORT, G. *Personality. A psychological interpretation.* New York: Henry Holt, 1937.

2. APTER, N. S., EISELE, C. W., McCULLOUGH, N. B., AND HALSTEAD, W. C. Cerebral pathology in brucellosis. *Trans. Amer. neurol. Assoc.,* 1948, **73**, 39-41.

3. APTER, N. S., HALSTEAD, W. C., EISELE, C. W., AND McCULLOUGH, N. B. Impaired cerebral functions in chronic brucellosis. *Amer. J. Psychiat.,* 1948, **195**, 361-366.

4. APTER, N. S., HALSTEAD, W. C., AND HEIMBURGER, R. F. Cerebral complications in essential hypertension. *Trans. Amer. neurol. Assoc.,* 1949, **74**, 219-222.

5. APTER, N. S., HALSTEAD, W. C., ALVING, A. S., TALSO, P. J., AND CASE, T. J. Alterations of cerebral functions in pheochromocytoma. *Neurol.,* 1951. To appear.

6. BEACH, F. A. *Hormones and behavior. A survey of interrelationships between endocrine secretions and patterns of overt response.* New York: Paul B. Hoeber, 1948.

7. BINET, A., AND SIMON, T. *The intelligence of the feeble-minded.* Baltimore: Williams & Wilkins, 1916.

8. BROWN, J. F. *The psychodynamics of abnormal behavior.* New York: Mc-Graw-Hill, 1940.

9. BRUNSWIK, E., AND REITER, L. Eindruckscharactere schematisierte. *Gesichter. Ztschr. f. Psychol.,* 1937, **142**, 67-134.

10. GOLDSTEIN, K. *The organism. A holistic approach to biology derived from pathological data in man.* New York: American Book, 1939.

11. HALSTEAD, W. C. Brain injuries and the higher levels of consciousness. In *Trauma of the central nervous system.* Assoc. Research Nerv. & Ment. Dis., Proc., 1943. Baltimore: Williams & Wilkins, 1945. Chap. XX.

12. HALSTEAD, W. C. A power factor (P) in general intelligence: the effects of brain injuries. *J. Psychol.,* 1945, **20**, 57-64.

13. HALSTEAD, W. C. *Brain and intelligence. A quantitative study of the frontal lobes.* Chicago: Univ. of Chicago Press, 1947.

14. HALSTEAD, W. C., AND WEPMAN, J. M. The Halstead-Wepman aphasia screening test. *J. Speech & Hear. Dis.,* 1949, **14**, 9-15.

15. HALSTEAD, W. C. (ed.) Brain and behavior; a symposium. *Comp. Psychol. Monogr.,* **20** (103). Berkeley: Univ. of California Press, 1950.

16. HALSTEAD, W. C. Frontal lobe functions and intelligence. *Bull. Los Angeles neurol. Soc.,* 1950, **15**, 205-212.

17. HEBB, D. O. The effect of early and late brain injury upon test scores, and the nature of normal adult intelligence. *Proc. Amer. phil. Soc.*, 1942, **85**, 275-292.

18. HILGARD, E. R. *Theories of learning.* New York: Appleton-Century-Crofts, 1948.

19. HIMWICH, H. E. *Brain metabolism and cerebral disorders.* Baltimore: Williams & Wilkins, 1951.

20. JAMES, W. *The varieties of religious experience.* New York: Longmans Green, 1902.

21. KLUCKHOHN, C., AND MURRAY, H. A. (eds.) *Personality in nature, society, and culture.* New York: Alfred A. Knopf, 1948.

22. LEWIN, K. *A dynamic theory of personality.* Trans. by D. K. Adams and K. E. Zener. New York: McGraw-Hill, 1935.

23. MURPHY, G. *Personality. A biosocial approach to origins and structure.* New York: Harper, 1947.

24. NIELSEN, J. M. *Agnosia, apraxia, aphasia* (2nd ed.). New York: Paul B. Hoeber, 1946.

25. SAMUELS, M. R. Judgments of faces. *Charact. & Pers.*, 1939, **8**, 18-27.

26. STERN, W. *General psychology from the personalistic standpoint.* Trans. by H. D. Spoerl. New York: Macmillan, 1938.

27. THORNDIKE, E. L., BREGMAN, E. O., COBB, M. V., *et al. The measurement of intelligence.* New York: Teachers College, Columbia Univ., 1927.

28. WILSON, D. P. *My six convicts. A psychologist's three years in Fort Leavenworth.* New York: Rinehart, 1951.

A Theoretical Model for Personality Studies

ANDRAS ANGYAL

Boston, Massachusetts

IN THIS PAPER I shall not discuss the question whether model building is fruitful or not in the study of personality; valid arguments in favor of such a procedure are adequately covered by other contributions to this symposium. Neither will I argue the comparative merits and disadvantages of the various types of model that have been or may be employed in this field. Instead I shall present a particular model which I have advocated previously for the formulation of a theory of personality (1), reformulating certain aspects of this theoretical orientation and illustrating my points with pertinent examples taken mainly from the field of psychotherapeutic theory and practice.

Personality may be described most adequately when looked upon as a unified dynamic organization—dynamic, because the most significant fact about a human being is not so much his static aspect as his constituting a specific *process:* the life of the individual. This process, the life of the person, is an organized, patterned process, a Gestalt, an organization. A true organization presupposes an organizing principle, a unifying pattern. All part processes obtain their specific meaning or specific function from this unifying over-all pattern. Therefore, it seems plausible that a tentative phrasing of the nature of this total pattern—the broad pattern of human life —may serve as an adequate model for the formulation of the problems pertaining to the study of personality.

The over-all pattern of personality function can be described from two different vantage points. Viewed from one of these vantage points, the human being seems to be striving basically to assert and to expand his self-determination. He is an autonomous being, a self-governing entity that asserts itself actively instead of reacting passively like a physical body to the impacts of the surrounding world. This fundamental tendency expresses itself in a striving of the person to consolidate and increase his self-government, in other words to exercise his freedom and to organize the relevant items of his world out of the autonomous center of government that is his self. This tendency—which I have termed "the trend toward increased autonomy"—expresses itself in spontaneity, self-assertiveness, striving for freedom and for mastery. In an objective fashion this tendency can be described as follows: the human being is an autonomous unit that, acting upon the surrounding world, molds and modifies it. His life is a resultant of self-determination on the one hand, and the impacts of the surrounding world, the situation, on the other. This basic tendency, the trend toward increased autonomy, expresses the person's striving from a state of lesser self-determination (and greater situational influence) to a state of greater self-determination (and lesser situational influence).

Seen from another vantage point, human life reveals a very different basic pattern from the one described above. From this point of view, the person appears to seek a place for himself in a larger unit of which he strives to become a part. In the first tendency we see him struggling for centrality in his world, trying to mold, to organize, the objects and the events of his world, to bring them under his own jurisdiction and government. In the second tendency he seems rather to strive to surrender himself willingly, to seek a home for himself in and *to become an organic part of something that he conceives as greater than himself.* The superindividual unit of which one feels oneself a part or wishes to become a part, may be variously formulated according to one's cultural background and personal understanding. The superordinate whole may be represented for a person by a social unit—family, clan, nation, by a cause, by an ideology, or by a meaningfully ordered universe. In the realm of aesthetic, social, and moral attitudes this basic human tendency has a central significance. Its clearest manifestation, however, is in the religious attitude and religious experience.

I wish to state with emphasis that I am not speaking here about a tendency which is an exclusive prerogative of some people only, e.g., of those with a particular religious bent or aesthetic sensitivity, but of a tendency that I conceive as a universal and basic characteristic in all human beings.

These two tendencies of the human being, the tendency to increase his self-determination in his expanding personal world, and the tendency to surrender himself willingly to a superordinate whole, can be summed up by saying that the human being comports himself *as if he were a whole of an intermediate order.* By this I mean a "part-Gestalt," like, for example, the cardiovascular system, or the central nervous system, each of which is a *whole,* an organization of many parts, but at the same time a *part* with regard to its superordinate whole, the body. The human being is both a *unifier,* an organizer of his immediate personal world, and a *participant* in what he conceives as the superordinate whole to which he belongs.

The basic human attitude that makes man behave as a part of a larger whole reflects itself also in his "horizontal relationships," that is in his relationship to the other "parts," to other persons. Were man's behavior determined exclusively by his urge for mastery, his attitude toward others could be only as toward means to his ends. Experiencing others as co-participants in a larger whole brings, however, another facet of his nature into manifestation. To avoid the coining of some outlandish term, we call this basic relation "love." In common usage this word has been badly misused to denote not only cheap sentimentality, but even relationships that are actually founded on exploitation, possessiveness, helplessness, and similar destructive attitudes. The basic nature of love consists in a recognition of the *value* and acceptance of the *otherness* of the loved "object" while at the same time one experiences an essential *sameness* that exists between oneself and what one loves.

To recognize and to accept the otherness of a person means to respect him as a valuable being in his own right, in his independence. This attitude is incongruous with any idea of possessiveness or any tendency to use him as means to an end, be this in the form of exploitation, domination, possessiveness, or some other attitude. In other words, it is incongruous with the nature of love to try to reduce the loved person to "an item in one's personal world," or to try to make him comply with one's demands, or to try to exert power over him in whatever way. Love has to be recognized as a basic human attitude which is quite distinct from and irreducible to man's self-assertive tendencies.

The recognition and acceptance of the otherness of the person implies, furthermore, an *understanding* of him. There can be no real love without understanding of the other person, only some sort of deceptive feeling based on an illusion. One does not recognize the otherness of a person as a reality by projecting into him one's fantasies, however flattering they may be. And when one sees in a person one's mother or father or anyone else, one ignores the person as he really is. In the last analysis this is a fundamental disregard for and destructive attitude toward the other person. The understanding of the other person—as we are now using this expression—is not some sort of shrewd "practical psychology" which has a keen eye for the weakness of people, but a deep perception of the core, of the essential nature of the other person. In love this essential nature of the other person is experienced as a value, as something that is very dear to one. Love is not "blind" but visionary: it sees into the very heart of its object, and sees the "real self" behind and in the midst of the frailties and shortcomings of the person.

Love has a second basic component which is complementary to respect for the otherness of its object: the experience of a certain fundamental belongingness and *sameness* between lover and the loved. Experientially, this is not "identification," that is, an identity that is more or less artificially created, but an existing identity that is *acknowledged*. Man behaves in certain fundamental respects *as if* he were a part, a shareholder in some kind of superordinate unit, in some kind of commonwealth. When two persons love one another they clearly or dimly have the feeling that something greater is involved therein than their limited individualities, that they are one in something greater than themselves or, as the religious person says, they are "one in God."[1]

Without such an implicit orientation all interests of a person would be centered in himself alone as an individual. He as an isolated entity would be facing an alien world and his reaching beyond himself would be only to possess, master and govern the surrounding world. He would compete with other people or he would calculatingly co-operate with them, but he would not love them. In

[1] This statement does not have to be understood in a theological sense. In this context it is not our concern, e.g., whether or not the "superordinate whole" is reality or not; we state only that man appears to function *as if* he were or would experience himself as a part of a superordinate whole.

order to love it is essential that a man come out of his shell, that he transcend his individuality, that he "lose himself." Somehow this self-abandonment is the precondition to a broadened existence in loving. One rejoices in the characteristic ways, in the real being, beyond the surface of pretense, of the other; one suffers in the other's misfortunes and in his misdeeds: therein one gains a whole new life with its joys and sorrows. One is enriched through a vital participation in another life without wanting, however, to possess the other person. The significant truth is expressed in the paradox that the one "who loses his life [of isolation], will gain it [in a broadened existence]." The paradox is resolved by recognizing that man functions as a part of a large whole. He has a life as a part—and that is all he has, as long as he remains in his self-enclosure. But it is possible for him to have a greater life, the life of the whole, as it is manifested in himself, in the other "parts," and in the totality.

I have described the over-all pattern of personality functioning as a two-directional orientation: *self-determination* on the one hand and *self-surrender* on the other. The first is the adequate attitude toward the items within one's individual world, the second, toward the greater whole toward which one behaves as a part. A particularly important aspect of this second orientation is the "horizontal" relatedness of the parts to other parts within the whole. I spoke in some detail of love because I believe—largely in agreement with current clinical views—that this is the very crux of the entire problem of personality and of interpersonal relationships.

Actual samples of behavior, however, cannot be ascribed exclusively to one or the other orientation. It is only in the counterfeit, the unhealthy, behavior that one or the other of these basic orientations is partially obliterated; in a well-integrated person the behavioral items always manifest both orientations in varying degrees. Instead of conflicting, the two orientations complement each other. As in the tendency toward increased autonomy one strives to master and govern the environment, one discovers that one cannot do this effectively by direct application of force, by sheer violence, but can do it by obedience, understanding, and respect for the laws of the environment—attitudes that in some way are similar to those of loving relationships. Similarly: bringing one's best to a loving relationship requires not only capacity for self-surrender but also a degree of proficient mastery of one's world, resourcefulness and self-reliance, without which the relationship is in danger of deteriorating into helpless dependency, exploitation, possessiveness, etc.

The central point of the model which we suggest here for the study of personality is the assumption that the total function of the personality is patterned according to a double orientation of self-determination—self-surrender. In the study of personality, as in any other scientific field, model building has its sole justification in its practical applicability, that is in its suitability for interpretation of the pertinent phenomena and for the formulation of meaningful problems. I have chosen the problem of the neuroses as a testing ground and I hope to demonstrate that the suggested model is useful for clarification of pertinent problems. Needless to say, only a few outstanding aspects of this broad field can here be touched upon, but this consideration may suffice to give a first impression as to the usefulness of the suggested frame of reference.[2]

I suggest the following thesis: The backbone of neurosis consists in a disturbance of the two basic tendencies that we have assumed as forming the over-all pattern of personality functioning. The two cardinal disturbances on which the neurosis rests consist, first, in the person's *loss of mastery* over his own fate, and second, what is rather generally accepted as a basic factor in the neuroses, namely *anxiety*. Loss of mastery is another expression for impairment of capacity for self-determination; anxiety, as we will try to show, is related to the impairment of the capacity for self-surrender and the capacity for love. These points may be best demonstrated by quickly surveying some of the crucial points in the development of a neurosis.

Although we have only vague and inferential knowledge of the infant's subjective experiences, there is sufficient evidence for assuming that his self and the world are not clearly distinguished, but rather blend into a single totality. This differentiation may be near zero in the prenatal life; it is small in the early days of infancy and usually is not quite complete even in adulthood—witness ubiquitous

[2] This nucleus of a model can be broadened and made more detailed. I have made efforts in this direction in the previously quoted book and also in (2).

wishful thinking and other autistic phenomena. The gradual birth of individuality may be largely a matter of maturation, but it is also stimulated and precipitated by *painful* contacts with the surrounding world. The hurtfulness of some objects of the environment and their frustrating resistance and independence in regard to one's wishes, so to say their disobedience, are impelling experiences to the recognition of their otherness.

These pains and frustrations—even the pain of being born into an uncomfortable world—are possibly not traumatic in themselves. Their chief significance seems to lie in their hastening both the birth of individuality and the experience of an outside world that is distinct from oneself. And with the birth of individuality the stage is set, the *human situation* is created. Here for the first time the opportunity is given to the person to manifest and unfold his essential nature. The experience of separateness from the surrounding world, which is governed by forces outside oneself, supplies the impetus to strive for mastery over the environment. At the same time, the experience of oneself as a separated, limited individual gives one the feeling of incompleteness and the urge to seek for a larger life to be part of and to participate lovingly in other lives. The experience of one's separateness represents both the necessity and the opportunity for the person to manifest his basic tendencies.

The real traumatising factors are those which prevent the person from expressing these basic tendencies. In the neurotic development there are always a number of unfortunate circumstances which instil in the child a self-derogatory feeling. This involves on the one hand a feeling of weakness which discourages him from the free expression of his wish for mastery, and on the other hand a feeling that there is something fundamentally wrong with him and that, therefore, he cannot be loved. The whole complicated structure of neurosis appears to be founded on this secret feeling of worthlessness, that is, on the belief that one is inadequate to master the situations that confront him and that he is undeserving of love.

The traumatising circumstances which condition this loss of self-confidence and of self-respect are many. They have been rather carefully explored by therapists who deal with neuroses. It will be sufficient here to call to mind some of the most common factors.

(A) The *over-protective attitude* of an insecure, anxious parent tends to convey to the child a feeling that he lives in a world that is full of dangers, and with which he is inadequate to cope. When a parent does too much for the child, he is telling him by implication that he is incapable of doing things by himself.

(B) When the parent is too eager for the child to do well and is *excessively critical* of him, he is likely to instil in the child the feeling "something must be very wrong with me; I can't do anything right."

(C) When parents distort and exaggerate the child's achievement, when they cast him into a *superior role* and have great expectations of him, they plant the seed of self-derogation in still another way. Deep down the child knows that the parents' picture of him is untrue, and measuring himself by these excessive and often fantastic standards, he secretly begins to feel utterly worthless.

(D) The too many "don'ts" which the child hears tend to create in him the feeling that those things which he *most wants* are the things that are forbidden and *evil*. This easily can give rise in him to a secret conviction that he is a fundamentally evil person.

(E) The ways in which children are being treated without *understanding* and without *respect* are many, and these are likely to create in the child the feeling that he just doesn't matter in this adult world, that he is of no account, that he is worthless. Often one wonders why the child accepts the verdict that he is worthless, instead of blaming the parent for being so obviously lacking in understanding, so wrong and selfish. The answer suggests itself that the child needs so much to feel that he has "good parents" that he tenaciously adheres to this belief and would rather assume himself to be evil or worthless than give up the idea that he has good parents.

The whole complex of self-derogation can be roughly—and admittedly somewhat artificially—divided into a feeling of inadequacy and the feeling of being unloved. The first leads to an impairment of self-determination, the second to the impairment of the capacity to love.

One important way in which the self-determination of a person may be impaired is his trading the birthright of mastery over his own destiny for the mess of pottage of protection—and dependency. In addition to the assumption of his weakness, an overvaluation of the power of his parents and of the protection which they can give induces the child to make this fatal bargain. The terms of the bargain are set, at least by implication: "You are weak and helpless against the world which is full of dangers; if you are good, if you do what we want you to do, and don't follow your impulses, we will take care of you and protect you."

Another circumstance that may induce a child to give up or

"escape" from his freedom is the exploitation by the adult of the child's loving nature. This is often done by holding up to the child the suffering his behavior may cause to others: "You may do it if you want to, but mother will be hurt"; or more directly: "What you do shortens my life"; "You put another nail in my coffin," etc. Particularly vicious and destructive is the influence of the "self-sacrificing mother," who holds up to the child the many sufferings, deprivations and unhappinesses which she has had to endure for the child, implying the tremendous ingratitude that a self-assertion of the child against her wishes would mean.

In response to these and similar emotional insults the child is gradually led to deny himself, to hide his spontaneous impulses—which he assumes to be evil—and to pretend to be or to try to be someone else, a more impressive and a more desirable person. This step is literally suicidal, and it is born out of an extreme despair. Indeed, only an extreme despair of any possibility to live in reality can induce a person to content himself with appearances, with the impression he makes. The exaggerated importance and value given to any external trappings with which a person may decorate himself is equivalent to declaring one's naked self worthless. If one basks in some sort of reflected glory, one declares one's real being to be ignominious.

All these various roads lead to loss of spontaneity, initiative, and genuineness. The child loses originality, which should not be the privilege of a few, but a rightful heritage of everyone. The neurotic person experiences himself as a straw in the wind who cannot act under his own power but has to *wait for things to happen,* who is a "victim of circumstances" and whose fate depends on good or bad "breaks."

The discussion of another basic disturbance, the impairment of the person's capacity to love, leads us into the problem of anxiety, which we should now briefly consider. It seems to me that the original word-meaning that suggests constriction, being narrowed in *(Beengung),* expresses best the essential nature of anxiety. A person who feels weak and unlovable and surrounded by a very alien and unfriendly world, will draw in his feelers and will surround himself with some protective shell. This shell, however, limits him and narrows him in to such an extent that he can barely move or breathe. We propose to define anxiety as this condition of the person. It seems preferable to use the term in this sense, as a "psycho-physically-neutral" term (William Stern), denoting a condition of the person which may or may not be consciously experienced. This usage would avoid the confusing issues of unconscious anxiety and such manifestations of anxiety that are conscious but not characterized by anxious feelings. Anxiety is not a mental phenomenon but a state of limitation of life. When we have sufficient information about a person's mode of living, we can determine whether his life is a narrowed one or not; that is, we can determine the presence and degree of the condition of anxiety, independently of the presence and degree of anxious feelings.

Anxiety is dynamically related to fears in a twofold manner: it is born out of fears and it leads to fears. It is fear that makes the person erect his defenses with the resultant state of constriction or anxiety. The person's impulses, however, rebel against the enclosure, against the limitation, and threaten to break through the wall of defenses. This threat from within is experienced in those nameless fears, fears without a conscious object, which one usually refers to as "anxiety."

This narrowed-in condition of anxiety paralyzes the effectiveness of the person in dealing with his environment. He does not really dare to venture into the outside world, but looks out upon it from behind his defenses with suspicion, fear, apprehension, envy, and hatred. The most destructive aspect of anxiety, of this self-enclosure, is, however, the loss of the capacity or rather the loss of the freedom to love. For love presupposes that instead of anxiously standing watch over one's safety, one dares to go out of oneself, to abandon oneself, to venture out in order to participate in the life of others and in a larger life of which he feels himself a part. It is the nature of the human being that he finds fulfilment only in a broadened existence, and that for him life confined to the limits of one's individuality in segregation from others is worthless. He can find happiness and peace only if he loves, that is, participates in life outside the confines of his individuality; and if he is loved, that is, received into and held fast and dear by another life.

Summing up this sketch of the origin of the neuroses, we have assumed that certain traumatising experiences create in the child a derogatory picture, a feeling of the worthlessness of his self. This feeling of worthlessness has two components: first, the feeling that one is inadequate, too weak to cope with the environment; and second, the feeling that one is unloved and unworthy of love. These then lead to an impairment of the person's self-determination on the one hand, and to anxiety with the loss of capacity to love, on the other. Neurosis represents a complicated interlocking system of maneuvers that are designed to maintain life in a human sense in spite of the fact that the person is wounded at the very core of his nature. This hypothesis of the origin of the neurosis I believe is more in agreement than at variance with many of the current views on the subject.

This view is also in good agreement with certain current theories of therapy. There are several psychotherapeutic factors to which, in general, a particularly important curative effect is ascribed. We shall mention only two such factors for further illustration of the main points of this paper: first, the patient's expression of anger in the therapeutic setting, and second, the positive relationship of the therapist to the patient.

The expression of angry feelings toward the therapist is assumed to have a beneficial therapeutic effect on the patient. This expression should be, however, more than just "blowing off steam," a catharsis. The patient's experience that he can express anger toward the therapist without being rejected or punished for it—important as it is—is not in itself the crucial therapeutic experience, but only preparatory to it. On the basis of a series of observations I am persuaded that not all forms of angry expressions are therapeutically valuable, but only certain kinds with well-defined differential characteristics. An outburst of anger, if it is not more than a blind expression of impotent rage, does not produce therapeutic effects, but is likely to leave the patient ashamed and guilty and worse off than before. The therapeutically effective anger is always a courageous expression and often clearly expresses the feeling that one would rather die than continue to live in fear and trepidation, tolerate injustice, etc. Such anger says emphatically: "I won't stand for it!" Daring to take this final aggressive stand makes one regain respect for oneself. And therein lies the therapeutic effect of this type of anger: it tends to abolish the feeling of inadequacy which is one component of self-derogation and which in turn is the foundation for the neurosis.

Even more fundamental is, however, the therapist's persistent attitude toward the patient, expressed in respect for him as a person of value, in understanding, in confidence that the patient can be saved, in sincere desire and devoted effort to help him to live a happier life. When the patient reaches the point of being able to trust the sincerity of the therapist's attitude, he will no longer be able to uphold completely the fiction of being unloved and unworthy, undeserving of love. And with this the other foundation of his neurosis begins to crumble.

The above examples, taken from the dynamics and therapy of the neuroses, may serve to illustrate the degree of usefulness and applicability of the model that was proposed here for the study of personality. It is not claimed that this brief exposition proves anything definitely, but perhaps it is sufficient to give a first impression of an avenue of approach which may be worth while to follow.

REFERENCES

1. ANGYAL, A. *Foundations for a science of personality.* New York: Commonwealth Fund, 1941.
2. ANGYAL, A. The holistic approach in psychiatry. *Amer. J. Psychiat.,* 1948, **105**, 178-182.